Finding God

Our Response to God's Gifts

*As I open this book, I open myself
to God's presence in my life.
When I allow God's grace to help me,
I see with truth, hear with forgiveness,
and act with kindness.
Thank you God, for your presence in my life.*

Barbara F. Campbell, M.Div., D.Min.

James P. Campbell, M.A., D.Min.

LOYOLA PRESS.
A JESUIT MINISTRY
Chicago

Imprimatur	In Conformity
In accordance with c. 827, permission to publish is granted on March 10, 2011 by Rev. Msgr. John F. Canary, Vicar General of the Archdiocese of Chicago. Permission to publish is an official declaration of ecclesiastical authority that the material is free from doctrinal and moral error. No legal responsibility is assumed by the grant of this permission.	The Subcommittee on the Catechism, United States Conference of Catholic Bishops, has found this catechetical text, copyright 2013, to be in conformity with the *Catechism of the Catholic Church*.

Finding God: Our Response to God's Gifts is an expression of the work of Loyola Press, a ministry of the Chicago-Detroit Province of the Society of Jesus.

Senior Consultants
Jane Regan, Ph.D.
Richard Hauser, S.J., Ph.D., S.T.L.
Robert Fabing, S.J., D.Min.

Advisors
Most Reverend Gordon D. Bennett, S.J., D.D.
George A. Aschenbrenner, S.J., S.T.L.
Paul H. Colloton, O.P., D.Min.
Eugene LaVerdiere, S.S.S., Ph.D., S.T.L.
Gerald Darring, M.A.
Thomas J. McGrath, M.A.

Catechetical Staff
Jeanette L. Graham, M.A.
Jean Hopman, O.S.U., M.A.
Joseph Paprocki, D.Min.

Grateful acknowledgment is given to authors, publishers, photographers, museums, and agents for permission to reprint the following copyrighted material; music credits where appropriate can be found at the bottom of each individual song. Every effort has been made to determine copyright owners. In the case of any omissions, the publisher will be pleased to make suitable acknowledgments in future editions. Acknowledgments continue on page 283.

Cover design: Loyola Press
Cover Illustration: Rafael López
Interior design: Loyola Press and Think Bookworks

ISBN-13: 978-0-8294-3174-2
ISBN-10: 0-8294-3174-8

LOYOLAPRESS.
A JESUIT MINISTRY

3441 N. Ashland Avenue
Chicago, Illinois 60657
(800) 621-1008

www.loyolapress.com
www.ignatianspirituality.com
www.other6.com

13 14 15 16 17 Web 10 9 8 7 6 5 4 3 2

Contents

Encounter
↓
→ *Session 1*
→ *Session 2*
→ *Session 3*

Session 6
→ *Session 4*

Session 6

iii

God, Our Creator and Father

Saint Jerome

Saint Jerome translated the entire Bible from Hebrew and Greek into Latin. He is the patron saint of librarians.

Saint Jerome

St. Jerome in his Study (oil on linen paper on panel), Jan van Eyck, (c.1390-1441).

"We must translate the words of the Scriptures into deeds; and instead of speaking saintly words, we must act them."

Jerome was born around A.D. 345 in what is now northern Italy. As a young man, he traveled and studied in the great European cities of Rome and Trier. He then went to live in the desert. While there, he said that he had "no other company but scorpions and wild beasts." He began to study Hebrew. He found the language difficult to learn, but his great effort was worth it. His knowledge of Hebrew made it possible for him to become a biblical scholar and translator.

In 382 Jerome began a huge task. He began to translate the entire Bible from the Hebrew and Greek texts into Latin. His endeavor took many decades and eventually produced a version of the Bible in the ordinary language of that time. Jerome's Latin translation of the Bible became the standard for use in the Church.

Jerome traveled to many places while working on his translation. He lived in Constantinople, Antioch, Alexandria, and Bethlehem. When war broke out and many refugees came to Bethlehem, Jerome took action. He knew that translating the Bible was not the only important task, so he gave up his work and study for a time to help people in need. He said, "We must translate the words of the Scriptures into deeds; and instead of speaking saintly words, we must act them." His feast day is September 30.

Think of Bible stories you know and enjoy. Share your favorite with the group.

The Bible, God's Story

Prayer

Loving God, help me to appreciate your Word in the Bible. Keep me faithful in praying from it so that I can come closer to you.

How the Bible Came to Be

The Bible is the Word of God. It is not just one book; it is a collection of many books. Different authors using different styles wrote these books. However, the Holy Spirit **inspired** them all. That is, although human beings wrote the Bible, the Holy Spirit guided them.

The Bible has two sections—the Old Testament and the New Testament.

The Old Testament

Jews wrote the Old Testament hundreds of years before Jesus was born. It tells the story of the Hebrew people and their faith in God. For example, the Book of Exodus tells the story of how Moses led the Hebrews out of Egypt and into the wilderness.

The New Testament

Just as the Old Testament is the story of the Jews, the New Testament is the story of the early Christians. Christians wanted to explain their new faith and teach others how to experience Salvation through Jesus. Some of the books are actually letters written by leaders such as Saint Paul. The most important books in the New Testament are the Gospels, which tell us about Jesus' birth, life, Death, and Resurrection. Although some of the Gospels tell the same stories, each expresses a unique point of view.

Did You Know?

The Old Testament includes 46 books. The New Testament includes 27 books.

Understanding the Bible

Sometimes the Bible is difficult to understand. Some passages are about events and people we know little about today. Other passages describe things that are difficult to understand because we do not think the same way people did long ago.

God has given the authority to interpret the Scriptures to the Catholic Church and the **Magisterium**—the pope and the bishops teaching together. Their **interpretation,** or explanation of the Bible, helps us avoid confusion and leads us to a better understanding of God's Word. Reading the Bible with the guidance of the pope and the bishops also makes it easier to learn about God's intention for us and for the salvation of the world.

When we read the Bible with the help of the Holy Spirit and the Church, we learn the meaning of God's revelation for our lives. This is especially true when we read about the words and actions of Jesus. The Church encourages us to read the Bible to learn about God, to grow in our relationship with him and others, to understand his message of love and forgiveness, and to teach a new generation what the Church believes.

Illuminated Bible page

Reading God's Word

Know this first of all, that there is no prophecy of scripture that is a matter of personal interpretation, for no prophecy ever came through human will; but rather human beings moved by the holy Spirit spoke under the influence of God.

2 Peter 1:20–21

GO TO PAGE 229

Inspiration and Guidance

Spend some time praying to the Holy Spirit. Think about how the Holy Spirit has inspired and guided those who wrote the Bible and the popes and bishops who have helped us understand it. Begin with this traditional prayer to the Holy Spirit.

Prayer to the Holy Spirit

Come, Holy Spirit, fill the hearts of your faithful.
And kindle in them the fire of your love.
Send forth your Spirit and they shall be created.
And you will renew the face of the earth.
Let us pray.

Lord,
by the light of the Holy Spirit
you have taught the hearts of your faithful.
In the same Spirit
help us to relish what is right
and always rejoice in your consolation.
We ask this through Christ our Lord.
Amen.

You have asked the Holy Spirit to fill your heart. The Spirit that renews the face of the earth can renew you as well. Ask the Holy Spirit to help you grow in understanding the Bible as you study it this year. Thank God for the gift of the Spirit and the grace and guidance always available to you. Rest quietly in God's presence, aware of his great love for you.

Making Choices

In the Book of Deuteronomy, Moses gives the Hebrews their final instructions before entering the Holy Land. Moses uses these words to urge the Hebrews to follow God's Law and make the right choice.

> I call heaven and earth today to witness against you: I have set before you life and death, the blessing and the curse. Choose life, then, that you and your descendants may live, by loving the LORD, your God, heeding his voice, and holding fast to him.
>
> *Deuteronomy 30:19–20*

If people want happiness in life, God's Law can give them the direction they need. They have to choose to follow God. He has given us free will to make choices. When we face tough decisions, we can pray to the Holy Spirit and read God's Word for help.

Seeking Advice

Think of a time when you had to make a serious choice and you asked an older, knowledgeable person for advice. How did that person help you? Write your ideas below.

_____

_____

_____

_____

_____

_____

_____

Living My Faith

Faith Summary

The Bible is God's revelation. By reading it, especially the stories of Jesus, we learn what God has done for us and how we can help others.

Words I Learned

inspired
interpretation
Magisterium
scriptorium*
Vulgate*

Ways of Being Like Jesus

Jesus was a Jew, and he studied the writings that now make up the Old Testament. *To understand what Jesus read and studied, read one or more of the following psalms from the Old Testament: 8, 84, 98, 114, and 150.*

Prayer

Thank you, God, for the Bible and all the ways it helps me learn about you.

With My Family

Activity A family Bible often contains a family history with information about births, deaths, and sacraments. Collect or update information by discussing your family history with an older relative. Write or type the information and keep it in your family Bible.

Faith on the Go Ask one another: *What is your favorite Bible verse, and why do you like it?*

Family Prayer Pray together the Prayer to the Holy Spirit.

* This word is taught with the Art Print. See page 229.

God Creates the World

Think of ways you can care for God's creation. Share your thoughts with the group.

Prayer

Creator God, help me learn to value people and all of creation as you do. Guide me to be true to you and myself so that I may be worthy of being made in your image.

The Book of Genesis

In Genesis we can read two stories about how God created the world.

The First Story of Creation

God spoke, and every part of the universe came into being—the sun and moon, the water and land, the plants and animals. God even made man and woman, and he made them in his own image. When he finished, he looked at everything and found that all of it was good.

adapted from Genesis 1:1—2:4

The writer of this story in Genesis wanted to make clear that God created every part of the world and that God saw everything as very good. Everything good in the Creation story includes all physical things, such as plants, animals, oceans, mountains, and rocks, as well as human beings. God was pleased with how everything turned out.

It's All Good

The first Creation story tells us that all of God's creation is good. Think of a plant, an animal, or some other aspect of creation that you believe has some negative qualities. Then, in the space provided, write what is good about it, rather than what is bad.

_____

_____

_____

_____

_____

Far from Home

The Jews were living in **exile** in Babylon when the first Creation story was written. They had been forced to leave their homeland to live in a place where the beliefs and customs were strange to them. Beliefs, customs, language, and dress make up a group's **culture.**

The Babylonians did not treat the Jews as equals. The Jews were discriminated against because of their ethnic origins. The word for this form of discrimination is *racism.*

The Babylonian culture was very different from the Jewish culture. Images of death and destruction caused by different gods filled the Babylonian creation stories. The Jewish creation story was peaceful and good. In their story God created the universe calmly with wisdom and love.

Babylonian monument honoring a priest from the ancient Temple of Marduk (900–800 B.C.)

Meet a Saint

Saint Frances Xavier Cabrini was born in Italy in 1850. Her devotion to missionary work eventually took her to the United States. While there, she helped establish schools, hospitals, and orphanages for Italian immigrants who were not treated well by society. She insisted that Italians living in the United States be treated the same way as everyone else. She is the patron saint of immigrants.

GO TO PAGE 230

God's Amazing Creation

Quiet yourself by taking a few deep breaths. Now imagine that you are in a completely dark place. You look all around, but you can see nothing. You hear the sound of splashing as you feel a gentle wind blowing over water. God is about to create the universe.

Bring into your mind images that you have seen of galaxies, planets, and stars. Enjoy the beauty of the many shapes and colors. Then imagine our solar system with the bright yellow sun, the giant planet Jupiter, and the delicate blue and green Earth. This is your home in the midst of this beautiful creation.

On Earth you see mountains, deserts, forests, rivers, and lakes. You see fish in the sea, birds in the air, animals that crawl, and animals that walk. God makes each one and says that each one is very good.

Finally look at the great expanse of humanity, people young and old, of many shades of skin color, harvesting crops, hunting, fishing, and building machines. God has made each one and called each one good.

Now spend some time giving thanks for the great variety in creation. In your own words, thank God for all that he has made. God has given all of this to you to care for. What promise can you make today that you will do your best to take care of his creation? Spend a few moments in God's awesome presence, aware of his care for all that he has created.

Equal in the Eyes of God

The story of Adam and Eve shows us a loving God who created man and woman—each a unity of body and soul—to be equal and to help God take care of the earth. When the man and woman disobeyed and rebelled against God, they had to leave his presence in the Garden of Eden. From then on life was different from the way God had intended it to be.

God created women and men as equals. Since the rebellion of Adam and Eve, history shows that women in many cultures have not been treated as equal to men. The word for this kind of discrimination is *sexism.* As Catholics we have a duty to oppose sexism, racism, and other forms of discrimination.

We Can Be Good

God made people to be good. Write three ways in which people can show their goodness.

1. _____

2. _____

3. _____

Draw a picture of yourself doing one thing that shows how God calls us to live.

Living My Faith

Faith Summary

God created the human family in his image and likeness. We reflect God's image by helping to care for the earth—its plants, creatures, and resources.

Words I Learned

culture   exile

racism   sexism

Ways of Being Like Jesus

Jesus understood that it was his responsibility to work with God to love people and care for the world. *Be kind to other people and care for God's creation.*

Prayer

God, thank you for making the earth a good place and for creating people to be good. Help me act in ways that show people that I am made in your image.

With My Family

Activity This week do something as a family to care for God's creation. Pick up litter in your neighborhood, plant a tree or flowers, or help at a local soup kitchen.

Faith on the Go Ask one another: *If you had to name your three favorite things that God created, what would they be?*

Family Prayer *Dear God, thank you for creating our family. Help us care for others as you care for us. Amen.*

Think of ways that you have shown trust in someone who cares for you.

Sin and Salvation

Prayer

God, my Creator, help me love and trust you so that doing what is right and avoiding anything that is wrong becomes my way of living.

Trusting God

When we stop trusting God, things start going wrong. In Genesis Chapters 3 and 4, we find two stories that show lack of trust.

Adam and Eve Disobey God

God placed Adam and Eve in the **Garden of Eden** and gave them everything they needed. Their life was very pleasant there. They tended the garden and cared for the animals, and they had each other for companionship. God told them that if they ate the fruit from one tree in the middle of the garden, they would die. It was the tree of knowledge of good and evil.

One day a snake convinced Adam and Eve that they were missing out on something. The snake said that they would not die if they ate from the tree but would have wisdom like God's. They forgot that God loved them and would tell them anything they needed to know. They did not need to disobey him by eating from the tree in order to be wise. They could walk and talk with God every day. Even so, Adam and Eve ate the fruit. That act of disobedience resulted in Original Sin. It changed everything. God sent Adam and Eve out of the garden. From that time on, life became more challenging for human beings.

adapted from Genesis 2:15–3:24

Stained-glass window depicting Adam and Eve, Sacred Heart Church, Faribault, Minnesota

Reading God's Word

I will put enmity between you and the woman,
   and between your offspring and hers;
He will strike at your head,
   while you strike at his heel.

Genesis 3:15

Cain and Abel

After leaving the garden, Adam and Eve had two sons, Cain and Abel. Cain and Abel had never known what it was like in the garden. They had never walked and talked with God as their parents had, so it's no surprise that Cain and Abel didn't get along. Most brothers argue sometimes, but Cain became so angry one day that he killed his brother, Abel.

God had mercy on Cain and allowed him to live, but he sent Cain away from home. Cain had his own family, and his children had families as well. As time passed, there were many people living in the world. By then Adam and Eve were dead, and no one remembered the garden. No one knew what it was like to walk and talk with God.

adapted from Genesis 4:1–16

Stained-glass window depicting Cain killing Abel, Trinity Lutheran, Valley City, North Dakota

Just a few years out of the garden and away from God's presence was all it took for people to start hurting one another. When people stop trusting God, they stop trusting one another as well.

God's Mercy

When do you need God's mercy? Maybe you have failed to do something you should have done. Complete these sentences.

When I disobey you by _____, Lord, have mercy.

When I need to _____, Lord, have mercy.

When I have trouble _____, Lord, have mercy.

When it is hard for me to _____, Lord, have mercy.

When I feel tired, afraid, angry, or _____, Lord, have mercy.

GO TO PAGE 231

Hail Mary

The disobedience of Adam and Eve resulted in Original Sin, but God did not give up on people. With the words of the angel to Mary, "Hail, full of grace," something new began. Mary gave birth to Jesus, who redeems and saves us. Pray the Hail Mary now, stopping to reflect on each sentence.

Hail Mary, full of grace, the Lord is with you.

God gave Mary the help she needed to accomplish what he called her to do. God also gives us the grace we need to live as Jesus wants us to live.

Blessed are you among women,
and blessed is the fruit of your womb, Jesus.

Mary was a person who was special because of her willingness to answer God's call in her life. God calls us each day to be a sign of his love in the world.

Holy Mary, Mother of God, pray for us sinners,
now and at the hour of our death.

Mary prays for our needs and the needs of the world. We ask her to support us as we present our own needs to God.

Take a moment to speak with Mary. Ask her to be with you as you present your needs before God.

Amen.

God's Mercy, Our Trust

Adam, Eve, and Cain made decisions that showed a lack of trust in God. Even though they sinned, God had mercy on them. In the story of Noah and the ark, God promised that he would never give up on us. We must always remember to place our trust in him.

Peruvian sculpture of Noah's ark

Words of Wisdom

These Bible verses teach us to put our faith and trust in the Lord. Read each verse and rewrite it in your own words.

Proverbs 3:5–6 _Trust in God. Follow the way of God_

1 John 1:9 _If you confess to God your sins, he will forgive them_

Jeremiah 17:7 _Trust in God, don't be rebellious to God's judgement. Don't try to be smarter than you are. Be humble_

Trust in the Lord

Write a poem that tells why you should trust in God. Use the letters of the word *trust* to begin each line of your poem.

T _____

R _____

U _____

S _____

T _____

Living My Faith

Faith Summary

The story of Cain and Abel shows how quickly people began to sin after Adam and Eve lost trust in God and disobeyed him. God renewed that trust through Noah and through his promise to help us even though we sin. When we trust God and obey his commands, we can avoid sin and live peacefully together.

Words I Learned

Garden of Eden

Ways of Being Like Jesus

After his baptism, Jesus was tempted. He resisted temptation by remembering God's commands in the Old Testament. *Rely on verses from the Scriptures to strengthen your faith in God.*

Prayer

God, thank you for not giving up on people, even though we often forget you. Let me listen to you every day and do what you prompt me to do.

With My Family

Activity Find an object that will remind your family of God's love and mercy. It may be a photograph, a statue, or any object that reminds you of a time when God took care of your family. Display this object in a prominent place in your home.

Faith on the Go Ask one another: *If you were to draw a picture to illustrate God's mercy, what would it look like?*

Family Prayer Pray together the Hail Mary.

Abraham Listens to God

What are some things that your parents ask you to do that are difficult for you?

Prayer

God, my Creator, over the years you have strengthened people's faith. Please strengthen mine now. You know what I need.

Sarah and Abraham Have a Child

The story of Sarah and Abraham takes place many years after Noah and the Flood, when the world had many people in it once again.

Abraham and Sarah had been married a long time, but they did not have children. One night God took Abraham outside and said, "Look up at the sky and count the stars if you can." He told Abraham that he would have as many descendants as there are stars in the night sky.

Years later Sarah had still not become pregnant. Then three visitors, sent from God, came to Abraham and Sarah. They said that in a year Sarah would have a son. Even though Abraham and Sarah thought they were too old to have children, Sarah gave birth to Isaac one year later.

adapted from Genesis 15:1–5; 18:1–10

Abraham and the Three Angels, Lodovicom Carracci, 1555–1619.

Abraham Is Tested

When Isaac was a young boy, God called out to Abraham and told him to kill Isaac and burn him on an altar. Abraham obeyed God's request and brought Isaac up a mountain, where he built an altar. As Abraham prepared to take his son's life, a messenger of God appeared and stopped Abraham just in time. God allowed Abraham to offer an animal instead of Isaac as a sacrifice.

adapted from Genesis 22:1–13

Why Did God Test Abraham?

The story of Abraham became a popular tale in Jewish culture at a time when sacrificing a firstborn child was a common practice in the area. In an attempt to criticize this practice, Jewish storytellers and writers offered this story in which God stopped Abraham from killing Isaac.

In the ancient world, the story of Abraham set Judaism apart from other religions. The story not only condemned child sacrifice but also provided a human model of the perfect Jew, Abraham, who was completely obedient and faithful to God. Abraham and Isaac are listed among the **patriarchs,** or founders of the Hebrew people, within ancient Israel. Patriarchs, along with prophets and other Old Testament characters, have been and always will be honored as saints by the Church.

Reading God's Word

Realize then that it is those who have faith who are children of Abraham.

Galatians 3:7

GO TO PAGE 232

Hope and Trust

Abraham and Sarah had reasons not to hope, yet God led them to increased faith and trust. Hope is an important Christian characteristic. We hope because we believe that God has made a commitment to us to care for us and show us how to live.

Pray the Act of Hope and think about your trust in God.

Act of Hope

*O my God, relying on your infinite mercy
    and promises,
I hope to obtain pardon of my sins,
the help of your grace,
and life everlasting, through the merits of
    Jesus Christ,
my Lord and Redeemer.
Amen.*

After you pray the Act of Hope, spend a few minutes with God. Thank him in your own words for his grace and for the hope that you will live with him forever. Rest a few moments in his presence.

Celebrating Ordinary Time

During the liturgical year, the Church remembers the life of Jesus, from the preparation for his coming and his birth (Advent and Christmas), through his Passion and Death (Lent and Holy Week), to his Resurrection and Ascension and the sending of the Holy Spirit to the apostles at Pentecost (Easter). During Ordinary Time we are called to follow Jesus every day.

The Church celebrates Ordinary Time twice during the year. Following the Christmas season and until Ash Wednesday is the first period. The second follows the Easter season and goes until the Advent season in late fall. Near the end of Ordinary Time, the Church celebrates All Saints Day and All Souls Day. The whole season of Ordinary Time lasts 33 or 34 weeks.

Ordinary time does not mean "common time," but rather "counted time." It comes from the word *ordinal* and refers to time in a certain order.

Prayer

Dear Jesus, please walk beside me each day of Ordinary Time.
Help me feel your presence and follow your lead at all times.

We Experience Scripture During Ordinary Time

Ordinary Time is a time to grow in our faith. We develop a deeper understanding of how Jesus wants us to live. We reflect upon and try to accept Jesus' invitation to love God, serve others, and avoid sin. We seek the presence of God's grace to help us grow in our understanding of Scripture. We thank him for the many opportunities he gives us to better hear, take to heart, and respond to the Word of God.

When we go to Mass on Sundays, we hear a reading from the Gospels. We are listening to the spoken Word of God. In the space provided, write a short prayer to pray silently after you hear the Gospel. Thank God for sharing his Word with you and ask him to help you better understand his message.

Dear God,

How Can I Grow?

During Ordinary Time we read Scripture to help us grow closer to God. Complete the following sentences.

During Ordinary Time I can read Scripture in order to _____

_____.

Reading Scripture makes me feel like _____

_____.

When I hear Scripture being read, I like to picture in my mind _____

_____.

Reading God's Word

Guide me in your truth and teach me,
    for you are God my savior.

Psalm 25:5

Mass During Ordinary Time

During Ordinary Time we hear Scripture readings that help us grow in our relationship with Jesus. The first reading is often about the Hebrews, our ancestors in faith. The second reading describes life in the early Christian communities. In the Gospel we hear about the life and ministry of Jesus.

What We Experience

Before the Gospel is proclaimed, we trace the Sign of the Cross on our forehead, mouth, and heart. We ask God, through his Word, to be in our thoughts, on our lips, and in our hearts.

Stained-glass window depicting Saint Mark as a lion at Trinity Church, Ripon, England.

Notice the Lectionary, the book containing the readings for Mass. If possible, look at its cover. You might see the symbols of the Gospel writers, or Evangelists: a winged man for Matthew, a winged lion for Mark, a winged ox for Luke, and an eagle for John. These symbols remind us of the richness of the Good News.

Symbols of My Faith

Draw a Christian symbol in the box to the right. On the lines below, explain the meaning of this symbol to you.

_____

_____

_____

_____

GO TO PAGE 233

Living My Faith

Faith Summary

Ordinary Time falls outside of the seasons celebrating specific aspects of the mystery of Christ. We celebrate Ordinary Time in two parts during the liturgical year. We use this time to help us grow in our faith and our understanding of Scriptures so that we can live the way Jesus wants us to live.

Ways of Being Like Jesus

Jesus blessed and broke bread at the Last Supper with his twelve apostles. *Pray before mealtime to thank Jesus for the many blessings he has given you.*

Prayer

Dear God, thank you for giving us this time to listen to your Word and grow closer to you every day. May we always feel the warmth of your light on our shoulders.

With My Family

Activity When you go to Mass during Ordinary Time, look for examples of the ideas and symbols you read about. Talk about what you see.

Faith on the Go Ask one another: *Why is reading Scriptures so important? How do you think it helps you grow closer to God?*

Family Prayer Use Ordinary Time to invite family members to grow in faith by keeping a prayer jar for special prayer intentions or requests.

Jesus, Our Lord and Savior

Saint John Neumann

John Neumann was one of the first American citizens to be declared a saint. He was also one of the founders of Catholic education in the United States.

Saint John Neumann

John Neumann was one of the most influential bishops to have lived in the United States. John was born in 1811 in Bohemia, which is now part of the Czech Republic. Although John studied for the priesthood in Bohemia, he was ordained in New York City. Soon after his ordination, Father John was sent to northwestern New York State, near Buffalo.

Many people in that part of the state were German, Irish, French, or Scottish immigrants. Father John knew eight languages, so he was able to communicate with his new parishioners. Over the years he served the people of New York, Pennsylvania, and Ohio. In 1852, in recognition of his wonderful work, Father John was appointed bishop of Philadelphia. While he was bishop, he established nearly 100 Catholic schools, wrote religious instruction books, including a children's catechism, helped those who were poor, and strongly encouraged devotion to Jesus Christ in the Blessed Sacrament.

John Neumann served as bishop of Philadelphia for eight years. He died suddenly in 1860 while leisurely walking along a city street. The Catholics of Philadelphia, especially new immigrants and those who were poor, mourned the loss of their spiritual leader. The Church honors him on January 5.

The Philadelphia Skyline, Pennsylvania.

God Is Faithful

In what ways does God work through someone you know to bring good into the world?

Prayer

Loving God, help me see your presence in all the ordinary events in my life.

Jacob Deceives His Brother

Jacob and Esau were twin brothers who competed with each other from the day they were born. Esau was born first—with Jacob holding onto his heel! The twins were nothing alike, in looks or personalities. Unfortunately their parents each favored a different son. Their father, Isaac, favored Esau. Their mother, Rebecca, favored Jacob. This likely worsened the competition between the brothers.

Esau was to receive the birthright—a special honor and inheritance passed from father to firstborn son—but Jacob wanted the birthright for himself. Esau returned home from hunting one day. He had not eaten and so was hungry. Jacob, who had been cooking, realized that this was his opportunity. He convinced Esau to trade his birthright to Jacob for a bowl of stew.

That wasn't the only time Jacob took advantage of Esau. When their father was near death, he wished to give his final blessing to Esau. Old and unable to see well, Isaac asked Esau to go hunting and bring back food for his favorite meal. While Esau was gone, Rebecca helped Jacob pretend to be Esau. Jacob tricked his father into giving the blessing to him instead. Esau became so enraged that he vowed to kill Jacob. Rebecca feared for Jacob's life and told him to flee to her brother Laban in Haran. Jacob never returned to his parents' home.

adapted from Genesis 25:19–34; 27:1–45

Link to Liturgy

During the Sign of Peace, the priest proclaims "The peace of the Lord be with you always." We respond "And with your Spirit." The priest then invites us to offer the sign of peace to others.

Jacob Is Tricked

Rachel meets Jacob at the well, Harold Copping, 1927.

Before fleeing to Haran, Jacob met with Isaac. He told Jacob to choose one of Laban's daughters as a wife. Shortly after arriving he met Laban's daughter Rachel. Jacob agreed to work for his uncle for seven years to win permission to marry her. He then learned what it was like to be on the receiving end of trickery. Laban switched daughters at the last minute, and Jacob mistakenly married Rachel's older sister Leah. Leah's face was covered with a heavy veil during the wedding. Jacob was heartbroken and still wanted to marry Rachel. In ancient Hebrew culture, men often had more than one wife. Laban agreed to let Jacob marry Rachel on one condition—Jacob had to work an additional seven years as payment. Over time God guided Jacob's destiny. He spoke to Jacob and reestablished the promise he had made to Abraham and Isaac. Then he gave Jacob the new name Israel. After that Jacob faced Esau, the brother he had tricked years before. Esau forgave Jacob, and their competition finally ended.

adapted from Genesis 29:15–30

Good Results from a Loving God

Jacob certainly had his flaws. He was ambitious and deceitful. He was a sinner, yet God had plans for Jacob. Even Jacob's mistakes could not ruin God's plans. Jacob's story is a good example of **Divine Providence**. Divine Providence is the way God's wisdom and love influence all he has created. As Jacob's story shows, God was able to bring about good results from bad choices. Both Jacob and his grandfather Abraham fulfilled God's plan, and their faith for him grew in the process.

GO TO PAGE 234

God Brings Good Results

God can bring about good results from our sins and mistakes, just as he did with Jacob. With this prayer you can offer God every part of your life, including your sins and mistakes.

Morning Offering

My God, I offer you my prayers, works, joys, and sufferings of this day in union with the holy sacrifice of the Mass throughout the world. I offer them for all the intentions of your Son's Sacred Heart, for the salvation of souls, reparation for sin, and the reunion of Christians. Amen.

Pray this prayer silently. When you come to the words "my prayers, works, joys, and sufferings," list in your mind some of those things. You may want to write them on paper and offer them to God.

Remember That God Loves You

God can take our sins and mistakes and bring about good results. But sometimes people may count on God to get them out of trouble when they deliberately do something wrong. This is never acceptable. Such an attitude does not come from real faith. It shows disrespect for God's love and patience.

Accepting Consequences

Read Jacob's stories again and list the consequences of his actions.

_____

_____

_____

_____

When we act in ways that hurt our friends or family members, feeling sorry and saying so may hardly seem enough. Sometimes we need to show that we are sorry. We've all heard the saying "Actions speak louder than words." This applies to our faith as well. Think of several actions you could take to show others that you are sorry. Write them below.

_____

_____

_____

_____

_____

_____

_____

Living My Faith

Faith Summary

Although Jacob was ambitious and deceitful, God still had a plan for him. Divine Providence can bring about good results from bad choices and situations.

Words I Learned

Divine Providence

Ways of Being Like Jesus

When Jesus needed to reflect on how God was working through him, he would spend time alone praying and listening to God. *Spend quiet time praying and thinking about how God works through you and the people you know.*

Prayer

Loving God, thank you for being faithful to me even when I sin. Help me trust in you through everything that happens to me.

With My Family

Activity Ask a family member to help you begin a "History of Our Family's Faith" scrapbook. Include photos of special events, information about relatives who have done religious work, and stories of answered prayers.

Faith on the Go Ask one another: *What are some events in your life that show God is faithful?*

Family Prayer Pray together the Morning Offering. Try to make it a part of your family's morning routine.

How does your family celebrate important events? Think about a celebration you took part in during the past year.

Passover and the Eucharist

Prayer

Faithful God, help me remember the sacrifice of Jesus when we celebrate the Eucharist. Help me to keep giving as Jesus did, even when it is a sacrifice for me.

God Leads a Nation to Freedom

During a time of terrible famine, Jacob's sons and their families moved to Egypt, hoping to find relief there. Jacob's son Joseph already lived in Egypt and was serving as an important government official. Jacob's family prospered in Egypt, and after many generations his descendants filled the country. God had given Jacob the name of Israel, and so his descendants came to be called **Israelites**. They were also known as Hebrews.

Long after Joseph's death, the **pharaoh**—Egypt's ruler—feared that the Hebrews had grown so great in number and strength that they might take over his country. To prevent this from happening, the pharaoh enslaved the Hebrews. They labored and suffered under Egyptian rule for nearly four centuries, but the Hebrews never gave up hope. They continued to pray to the God of Abraham, Isaac, and Jacob to save them, and God did hear their prayers. Responding to the cries of his Chosen People, God chose a man named Moses to lead them out of slavery. Moses was a Hebrew, but he had been brought up as the son of the pharaoh's daughter.

adapted from Exodus 1:1—2:10

Did You Know?

The pharaoh's daughter found Moses as a baby, in a basket floating on a river. She drew him out of the water and gave him the name Moses, which means "is born" in Egyptian. *Moses* is also similar to the Hebrew word that means "to draw out."

God Appears to Moses

Though he was raised as an Egyptian by the pharaoh's daughter, Moses knew he was a Hebrew. He felt great sympathy for the enslaved Hebrews. One day Moses observed an Egyptian abusing a Hebrew slave, so he intervened and killed the Egyptian. When the pharaoh learned what he had done, Moses fled the country. He settled in the land of Midian. While in Midian God appeared to him. Moses was tending a flock of sheep when he heard a voice coming from a bush. The bush was on fire, but the flames did not consume it. God said that he was the God of Abraham and Jacob and that he had come to set the Hebrew slaves free. Moses asked God's name. God responded in Hebrew, "**Yahweh,**" which means "I am who I am."

adapted from Exodus 2:11—3:17

The name Yahweh reinforces the Covenant that God made with the Hebrew people to be with them always. Today God makes his presence known to us through the Holy Spirit.

Moses Accepts His Mission

As with Jacob and Abraham, God had a plan for Moses. God chose Moses to lead the Hebrew people out of slavery. Moses was hesitant and concerned that he might not succeed at such a difficult task. When he finally accepted the mission, he knew he would have to trust God and follow his instructions. Moses returned to Egypt to convince the pharaoh to free the Hebrew slaves. The pharaoh was stubborn and did not believe that God would help the Hebrews. God had to perform many mighty wonders before the pharaoh would change his mind. The Passover was the last of these wonders. Today the Jewish people still celebrate Passover as a memorial to God for freeing them from slavery.

EXPLORE

GO TO PAGE 235

SESSION 7 • *Passover and the Eucharist*   41

Psalm 23

When we gather for the Eucharist, we remember how God leads and cares for his people. We give thanks. We commit ourselves to making the world a place where every person comes to the table to be restored in body and spirit.

Pray together Psalm 23 for your prayer today.

> The LORD is my shepherd;
>   there is nothing I lack.
> In green pastures you let me graze;
>   to safe waters you lead me;
>   you restore my strength.
> You guide me along the right path
>   for the sake of your name.
> Even when I walk through a dark valley,
>   I fear no harm for you are at my side;
>   your rod and staff give me courage.
> You set a table before me
>   as my enemies watch;
> You anoint my head with oil;
>   my cup overflows.
> Only goodness and love will pursue me
>   all the days of my life;
> I will dwell in the house of the LORD
>   for years to come.

Now spend a few minutes reflecting on God's goodness and love. Thank God in your own words for his guidance along the right path and the courage he gives you in difficult times.

Celebrating the Eucharist

Passover is still celebrated by Jewish people today as a memorial to God for freeing them from slavery. The Last Supper was a Passover meal that Jesus shared with his disciples before he was crucified. During that meal Jesus gave the gift of himself in the Eucharist for the very first time.

For Catholics, Mass is a memorial of Christ's Passover from death into new life. We celebrate Mass in remembrance of the covenant with God that began after Jesus' Death and Resurrection. In every Mass we celebrate the sacrifice that Jesus made to save humanity from sin. In the **Eucharistic liturgy,** Jesus' sacrifice becomes present to us as we share in his Body and Blood.

Painting of the Last Supper in St. Basil's Cathedral, Moscow, Russia.

A Family of Faith

The Eucharistic liturgy is the heart of our Catholic faith. The Eucharist strengthens and unites us as a community of faith. Describe two of your family's rituals or traditions. Tell how you think they strengthen and unite your family. On a separate sheet of paper, illustrate your favorite family ritual or tradition.

_____

_____

_____

_____

Did You Know?

Catholics throughout the world, including **Eastern Catholic Churches,** celebrate the Eucharist. All of us share the same apostolic tradition, honoring Jesus and the Covenant between God and his people.

Living My Faith

Faith Summary

During Passover Jews recall the night that God spared their children as he punished the Egyptians for enslaving the Hebrew people. Jesus' last meal was a Passover meal, but he added a new meaning to this meal, one that we celebrate in the Eucharistic liturgy.

Words I Learned

Eastern Catholic Churches	**Israelites**	**Sabbath***
Eucharistic liturgy	**pharaoh**	**Yahweh**

Ways of Being Like Jesus

Jesus performed many miracles during his life. On one occasion he turned a few loaves of bread into enough food to feed thousands. *Help to feed those in need by contributing to local food drives.*

Prayer

Thank you, Jesus, for helping us to understand God's covenant with us in a new way. You allowed your own blood to be shed so that we would be saved from sin.

With My Family

Activity When you participate in Mass with your family, pay special attention to the Eucharistic Prayer. After Mass discuss phrases and actions that stood out for you.

Faith on the Go Ask one another: *What is one thing you could sacrifice to help a person in need?*

Family Prayer *Thank you, Lord, for the gift of your Body and Blood in the Eucharist. Help us spread your message of love and sacrifice to others. Amen.*

* This word is taught with the Art Print. See page 235.

God Leads His People

Think about some of the trips you have taken—vacations, visits to friends and relatives, or trips to important places.

Prayer

Faithful God, lead me and guide me to be more committed to my journey of faith.

45

The Great Exodus

After the Passover the pharaoh could no longer refuse Moses's request to release the Hebrews from slavery. He recognized the incredible power of God and so allowed Moses and the Hebrews to leave Egypt. After hundreds of years of slavery, Moses and the Hebrews began their **Exodus**—a long journey—to freedom and the Promised Land.

The Israelites wandered in the desert for 40 years before they settled in the land of **Canaan**. They experienced great hardship and anxiety on their journey and lost their trust in God many times. They often complained to Moses for bringing them out of Egypt to die in the desert. They were frightened, but throughout their journey God provided everything they needed. He gave them **manna**—food that fell from the sky—and water where there was none to be found. He provided a cloud by day and a pillar of fire by night to guide them along the way.

adapted from Exodus 12:31—13:22

God Saves the Israelites

The most miraculous events of the Exodus occurred when the Hebrews crossed the Red Sea. After Moses and the Hebrews left Egypt, the pharaoh changed his mind and wanted to destroy them. He sent a grand army to pursue them. The Egyptian army closed in on the Hebrews, trapping them at the edge of the Red Sea. At that moment God told Moses to stand before the sea and raise his staff. As he did, the water parted and a path of dry ground stretched across to the other side.

Moses releasing the waters of the Red Sea, Bible illumination, 10th century.

Moses and his people crossed the sea on the dry path. The Egyptian army followed close behind until they realized that the Hebrews had God on their side. Then the Egyptians began to retreat, but before they could return to the shore, God told Moses to raise his staff again. As he did, the walls of water crashed down and destroyed the Egyptian army.

adapted from Exodus 14:5–14:31

Trusting God Through It All

Are you ready to trust God in difficult situations? Complete the sentences below to show your trust in God.

When I do not succeed at _____, I trust that God _____

_____.

When I feel _____, I trust that God _____

_____.

When I need _____, I trust that God _____

_____.

GO TO PAGE 236

Write a Personal Prayer

Moses trusted that God would help him lead the Hebrews out of Egypt. Write a prayer asking God to help you trust that he is always there to lead, guide, and protect you, no matter what the situation.

This is your personal prayer. Be creative!

_____

_____

_____

_____

_____

_____

Silently pray your prayer to yourself, knowing that you are in the presence of God.

Exploring the Ten Commandments

God gave Moses and the Hebrew people the Ten Commandments as instructions to have a good relationship with God. Rewrite each Commandment in your own words. You can rewrite negative statements to make them positive or vice versa. For example, after "You shall not steal," you could write "Be generous to others." You are not rewriting the Bible but rather exploring the meaning of these verses.

I am the Lord your God: you shall not have strange gods before me.

_____

You shall not take the name of the Lord your God in vain. _____

_____

Remember to keep holy the Lord's day. _____

_____

Honor your father and your mother. _____

_____

You shall not kill. _____

_____

You shall not commit adultery. _____

_____

You shall not steal. _____

_____

You shall not bear false witness against your neighbor. _____

_____

You shall not covet your neighbor's wife. _____

_____

You shall not covet your neighbor's possessions. _____

_____

Living My Faith

Faith Summary

God renewed his Covenant with Abraham by freeing the Hebrews from slavery and protecting them throughout their Exodus from Egypt.

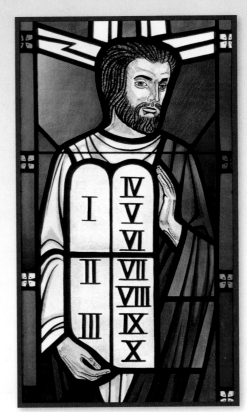

Words I Learned

Canaan

Exodus

manna

Ways of Being Like Jesus

Jesus knew that the Ten Commandments and the other teachings of the Old Testament were important. He added new meaning to our faith, but he did not set aside the faith of Abraham, Isaac, Jacob, and Moses. *Follow the Ten Commandments to be more like Jesus.*

Prayer

Dear God, thank you for helping me to find my way each day.

With My Family

Activity Sometime during this week, ask everyone in your family to help write 10 family commandments to follow. When you have decided on these commandments, display them in a place where everyone can see them.

Faith on the Go Ask one another: *In what ways can you show your trust in God?*

Family Prayer *Dear God, guide us to make good choices and follow your Commandments every day. Amen.*

Being Faithful to God

Think about all the choices you make each day. How do you tell the difference between a good choice and a bad choice?

Prayer

Generous God, show me how I can make good choices that will honor you.

51

Choices

There are many dramatic stories in the Old Testament. In Genesis we read about Noah and the great flood. In the Exodus story, God parted the Red Sea to save the Hebrews and then destroyed the Egyptian army. The Old Testament also tells personal stories about people who had to make difficult decisions that changed their lives. These stories help us understand why it is important to make good decisions in our lives. These stories also show us the consequences of making bad decisions. We all face times when we must make difficult decisions. Some of our decisions can have serious consequences. We can apply the lessons from these stories to the decisions we make. The stories of David and Ruth in particular show how moral choices can affect our relationship with God.

David, King of Israel

After the Exodus the Hebrews settled in Canaan and established a kingdom. David, their second king, united the various tribes under one rule and established **Jerusalem** as the capital. David's kingdom was prosperous, and the people approved of him. He was faithful and trusted in God. As David's power grew, however, his wisdom and ability to make good decisions did not. He became arrogant and used his power to get whatever he wanted.

David's arrogance eventually led him to make several bad decisions. He disrespected God's love and thought that he could do anything without having to face the consequences.

David's Choice

One day, while his army was away at war, David saw Bathsheba, the wife of Uriah, an army captain. David felt an instant attraction to Bathsheba and wanted to be with her.

David knew that it would be wrong to be with a married woman. Nevertheless, he became envious and resentful of Uriah for having what he wanted. David ultimately based his decision on envy and lust, rather than on his knowledge of right and wrong. He chose to be with Bathsheba while Uriah was away. By committing adultery, David broke one of God's Commandments.

When David had learned that Bathsheba was pregnant with his child, he tried to cover up his sin. He arranged for Uriah to be in the front lines of battle so that he would be killed. Uriah did die in battle, and David quickly married Bathsheba.

adapted from 2 Samuel 11:1–27

David's decisions broke two of God's important Commandments. Although God forgave David for his poor choices, he had to live with the awful consequences of his actions for the rest of his life.

Reading God's Word

Two blind men were sitting by the roadside, and when they heard that Jesus was passing by, they cried out, "[Lord,] Son of David, have pity on us!"

Matthew 20:30

GO TO PAGE 237

Prayer

Prayer of Forgiveness

We all need God's forgiveness for the bad choices we make. King David made some bad decisions, but deep in his heart he wanted to do what was right. He wanted to love God and be the person God wanted him to be. Psalm 51 is a prayer of forgiveness that highlights David's sorrow. Use the prayer adapted from Psalm 51 as a model to ask God for forgiveness.

Group A: *God, you have so much goodness and compassion. Please help me to put my sins and mistakes behind me. Wash away my guilt.*

Group B: *I know that I've done wrong and that I've sinned against you. I deserve the consequences of my actions.*

Group A: *Please give me a clean heart, one that wants to trust you and listen to you.*

Group B: *Give me greater strength to follow the right way, no matter what.*

Group A: *Please don't turn away from me because I've done wrong.*

Group B: *Help me to be happy again. Help me to enjoy being your child.*

Group A: *When you forgive me and help me, other people will see what it means to be a child of God.*

Group B: *Help me to say and do the things that will help other people have faith and avoid mistakes.*

All: *Thank you for your forgiveness, and for giving me a fresh start. Amen.*

Moral Decisions

Having freedom of choice, or free will, does not mean we can do anything we please. David's power clouded his judgment and ability to make good choices. God reminds us that choice is not only a gift granted to us but also a responsibility. We may not always find it easy to make good choices. Sometimes we cannot predict the consequences of our decisions. Even if the right moral choice is obvious, emotions such as envy, fear, and lust make it difficult to do the right thing.

David and Bathsheba in the garden

When we face moral decisions, it is important to remember the instructions of God and the Church. We should consider the consequences of our actions as well. Although we may not always make the right decisions, God offers forgiveness to those who seek it. We should keep in mind that, like David, we must live with the consequences of our choices for a long time.

Choice and Consequence

Think about a time when you had to make a difficult decision. Describe the situation and the things you considered during the decision-making process. If you had to choose again, would you make the same decision? What were the good or bad consequences of your decision?

_____

_____

_____

_____

_____

Faith Summary

Stories of moral choices in the Bible teach us how decisions can affect relationships with God and with other people in both positive and negative ways.

Word I Learned

Jerusalem

Ways of Being Like Jesus

Jesus knew that making the right moral choice was sometimes difficult. *Think about the consequences of important decisions and then act according to God's instructions.*

Prayer

Thank you, God, for giving us examples in the Scriptures of both good and bad choices. Help me learn from those stories to avoid making bad choices myself.

With My Family

Activity At dinner one night, lead your family in a discussion about the good decisions you have each made during the week and how you made them.

Faith on the Go Ask one another: *What can you do to ensure you make choices that improve your relationship with God?*

Family Prayer Dear God, remind us to always seek your help as we make difficult decisions. Amen.

Celebrating Advent

Advent is the season in the Church's liturgical year when we prepare for the celebration of Jesus' birth. During Advent we ask ourselves if we are living the life Jesus calls us to live. Advent is also a time of hope when we ask God to be with us as we prepare to welcome Emmanuel, which means "God with us."

There are four weeks in the Advent season. The first Sunday of Advent marks the beginning of the new liturgical year. On December 8, we celebrate the Immaculate Conception, a feast honoring Mary. The Advent season ends on Christmas Eve.

The word *Advent* comes from the Latin word *adventus*, which means "arrival" or "coming." Advent is a season of grace during which we prepare ourselves for the coming of Jesus.

Prayer

Dear God, thank you for giving us these four weeks to prepare to celebrate the birth of your Son. We are so thankful for all the people that help us along this path we're traveling to welcome Jesus.

We Reflect During Advent

Advent is celebrated with a spirit of reflection, anticipation, preparation, and longing. It is a time to reflect on the world as it was before the birth of Jesus, when God's people anticipated the coming of the promised Savior. The longing of God's people is shown in the prophecies of Isaiah.

> There shall be no harm or ruin on all my holy mountain; for the earth shall be filled with knowledge of the LORD, as water covers the sea. *Isaiah 11:9*

God's people looked forward to the time foretold in this Scripture. They were filled with hope and faith. Today we share in the same anticipation, hope, and faith.

We Are God's People

Whether we were born thousands of years before Jesus' birth or just 11 or 12 years ago, we are all God's people. As those born thousands of years ago anticipated the coming of the Lord, we prepare for the celebration of Jesus' birth and anticipate his second coming. On a separate sheet of paper, write a letter to a distant relative. Share what Advent means to you.

Reading God's Word

You too must be patient. Make your hearts firm, because the coming of the Lord is at hand. *James 5:8*

Mass During Advent

During Advent we hear readings from the Old Testament that tell about God's people as they await the Savior. Sometimes we hear readings from Isaiah that foretell Jesus' coming.

> But a shoot shall sprout from the stump of Jesse, and from his roots a bud shall blossom. The spirit of the LORD shall rest upon him: a spirit of wisdom and of understanding, A spirit of counsel and of strength, a spirit of knowledge and of fear of the LORD.
>
> *Isaiah 11:1–2*

In this passage the imagery of a blossoming bud from the stump of Jesse, David's father, foretells Jesus' coming and the miraculous things to follow.

What We Experience

During Advent the altar is draped with a purple cloth, and the priest wears purple vestments. Images in the stained-glass windows might depict the connection between the time before and after Jesus, and may include the prophets who foretold Jesus' birth.

Growing Closer to Jesus

Our reflections of ourselves and of the time before Jesus help us grow closer to him. Our friends, family, and parish can also help us grow closer to Jesus. Name two people in your life and describe how they help your relationship with Jesus grow.

1. _____ helps me grow closer to Jesus by _____

_____.

2. _____ helps me grow closer to Jesus by _____

_____.

GO TO PAGE 238

Faith Summary

The Church's liturgical year begins on the first Sunday of Advent. The season gives us time to prepare our celebration of Jesus' birth. We also think back to the time when God's people were awaiting the coming of the Savior. Just like the people of ancient times, we wait with hope for the coming of Jesus.

Words I Learned

Jesse Tree*

Ways of Being Like Jesus

Jesus forgave our sins. *Always be willing to forgive a friend or family member who has made a bad choice.*

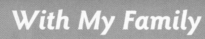

Prayer

Dear God, thank you for all the wonderful people you have placed in my life. Please shine your light upon us as we make our journey through the season of Advent.

With My Family

Activity When you go to Mass during Advent, look for examples of things described on the previous page. Talk about what you see.

Faith on the Go Ask one another: *In what ways can you welcome Jesus into your life?*

Family Prayer Use Advent as a time to send a letter to a relative who lives far away, saying that you remember him or her in your prayers.

* This term is taught with the Art Print. See page 238.

The Church, Our Community in the Spirit

Saint Helena

Helena lived during the third century A.D. in the Roman Empire. As the mother of the Roman emperor, she used her influence to build churches in holy cities such as Jerusalem.

Saint Helena

Helena was born during the third century A.D. in a part of the Roman Empire to the north of Italy. She came from a poor family and worked at her father's inn, where she met many travelers from all over the world. Helena married one such traveler, a general in the Roman Empire.

Marriage to a Roman officer changed Helena's life. Her husband soon became more than a general in the Roman army—he became the emperor of Rome. Helena, meanwhile, gave birth to a son and named him Constantine. After her husband's death, Constantine became the emperor, and he named his mother empress of Rome.

For 200 years Roman rulers had persecuted Christians. Under Constantine's rule the persecution ended. He allowed Christians to worship without fear. Helena became a devout follower of Jesus Christ and was baptized. She used her power as empress to help as many people as she could. After visiting Bethlehem and Jerusalem, Helena ordered that churches be built in the holy cities so that people could come to pray.

Helena could have done many selfish things in her privileged position, but she chose to use her power to help those who followed Jesus Christ. The Church honors Saint Helena on August 18.

Describe a place that makes you feel as if God were right there beside you.

God's Presence in the Temple

Prayer

Loving God, give me the grace to know your presence and to help other people to welcome you into their lives.

The Ark of
the Covenant

Solomon's Temple

For many years King David had dreamed of building a great temple to honor God.
He had set aside materials to build it and had plans for its design. God, however,
had other plans and chose David's son, Solomon, to fulfill that dream. After David's
death, Solomon, now the king, enlisted thousands of men to begin construction of
a temple on Mount Zion—a tall hill in Jerusalem.

Since the Exodus from Egypt, the Hebrews had worshiped God in a tent. They had
to set up the tent and then tear it down as they traveled across the desert. The
tent contained the **Ark of the Covenant.** This large gold box is said to have held
the actual stone tablets with the Ten Commandments that Moses had received on
Mount Sinai.

The most talented builders and artists of the time designed and built the Temple—
all according to God's instructions. After seven years of work, the people finally
had a temple at the heart of their kingdom. Representatives of the entire kingdom
attended the dedication of the Temple. A grand procession carried the Ark of the
Covenant into the **Holy of Holies,** the most sacred room inside the Temple.
At the ceremony Solomon asked God to remember his promise to Moses—that
God would always be present among his people. Solomon also reminded the
people that God had continued to be faithful to them. He instructed them to
respond to God in their hearts and obey the commandments.

adapted from 1 Kings 6:1—8:26

God's Presence in the Temple

In ancient Judaism the Temple was an important part of life. People worshiped and celebrated feasts and festivals to recall God's faithfulness and to praise his holiness. Animal **sacrifices** were common at these ceremonies. Worshipers offered animals, and priests sacrificed them on an altar outside the central Temple building. Sacrifices were a concrete way for worshipers to offer thanks for all that God had provided.

Throughout the centuries people have understood God's presence in many ways. During the Exodus the Hebrews saw a cloud by day and a pillar of fire by night and believed that God was traveling along with them, guiding their way. Eventually they made a special tent, called a tabernacle, in which to worship God. Then Solomon built the Temple. God made his presence known through the priests, prophets, and kings. He called priests to offer sacrifices in the Temple. He called prophets to help people understand how he wanted them to care for one another. He called kings to care for the people and rule in a just way.

Sacred Site

Workers completed construction of Solomon's Temple on Mount Zion in 953 B.C. Although there are no archaeological remains, the Bible describes the Temple in great detail in I Kings 7:13–51. Two large bronze pillars rested on each side of the entrance, and the interior of the Temple was decorated with gold-plated wooden sculptures.

GO TO PAGE 239

Dwell in Us, O Holy Spirit

Just as the Hebrew people saw the Temple as the dwelling place of God, we believe that the Holy Spirit makes the Church "the temple of the living God." After Baptism we, too, become temples—sanctuaries in which the Holy Spirit may dwell. Imagine yourself in the presence of the risen Jesus. Silently pray these petitions. Pause after each one, look to Jesus within you, and ask him to make you a worthy temple of the Holy Spirit.

Make me beautiful with love and compassion that will bring healing to others.

℟. *Lord Jesus, make me a worthy temple of the Holy Spirit.*

Make me open, peaceful, and welcoming to all people.

℟. *Lord Jesus, make me a worthy temple of the Holy Spirit.*

Make me joyful, full of happiness that will give joy to others.

℟. *Lord Jesus, make me a worthy temple of the Holy Spirit.*

Make me truthful and just so that others know they can come to me for help and hope.

℟. *Lord Jesus, make me a worthy temple of the Holy Spirit.*

Now spend more quiet time with Jesus. Pray that he may always find a home in your heart. Ask him for what you need at this time. Rest in his presence, aware of his great love for you.

We Are the Church

Today we are all the Church because God dwells within us. The Holy Spirit helps us show God's presence and love to others through our actions. As the Church and the People of God, we are called to love others as God loves us. This means that we cannot discriminate against others on the basis of their background, race, sex, or beliefs. **Discrimination** can make people feel they are not good enough for God or that he does not love them.

The Sacrament of Holy Orders

We become members of the Church through Baptism. As Christians we share in the ministry of Jesus as priest, prophet, and king. The men called to receive the Sacrament of Holy Orders are visible signs of the priesthood of Jesus Christ. The Holy Spirit calls priests and bishops to offer the Sacrifice of the Mass and to serve as leaders in the Church. Deacons are called as visible reminders for Christians to serve one another as a king serves his people.

Write ways you can show others that you are the Church.

At home _____

_____

At school _____

_____

In your community _____

_____

Living My Faith

Faith Summary

The Temple in Jerusalem was a place where people could experience God's presence. After his Resurrection Jesus Christ sent the Holy Spirit to gather a new People of God, the Church, where God is present today.

Words I Learned

Ark of the Covenant   Holy of Holies

discrimination   sacrifices

Ways of Being Like Jesus

Jesus loved the Temple, and he treated it as his Father's house. *Respect your church, other people, and yourself as temples of the Holy Spirit.*

Prayer

Jesus, my guide, thank you for helping me to open myself to the Holy Spirit dwelling in my life.

With My Family

Activity What can your family display in your home to tell others that God dwells there? Ask your family members to help you find a place to display a piece of art or a picture showing that your home is a holy place.

Faith on the Go Ask one another: *If you saw someone discriminating against another person, what would you do?*

Family Prayer *Dear God, help us to honor ourselves and others as temples of your Holy Spirit.*

What is your favorite way to pray? What words do you use when you pray alone?

Psalms, the Prayers of Jesus

Prayer

Lord Jesus, help me learn to express to God my thanks, my needs, my sadness, and my joys by praying the psalms as you did.

A Prayer Collection

The Book of Psalms is a collection of 150 sacred songs and poems that are models for how we can pray. Many Catholics pray psalms every day in the **Liturgy of the Hours**—the official prayer of the Church. The Liturgy of the Hours includes specific prayers to say at different times of the day. The psalms help us unite our own feelings and situations with the prayers of the Church as a whole.

The most common types of psalms express praise, lament (sadness), thanksgiving, intercession (need), and wisdom. We can pray these simple and direct prayers at any time. The psalms call us to prayer and give us words to speak to God from our hearts.

Prayer Together and Alone

When we participate in Mass or other liturgies, we join in **communal prayer.** On these occasions we pray the same prayer or psalm together with other members of the Church. We share the experience of speaking with and listening to God. The Hebrew people also practiced communal prayer and used many of the psalms in this way.

Personal prayer is also very important. Personal prayers are our own conversations with God. Our spiritual life develops and our faith grows when we take time to be still and speak honestly with God.

Link to Liturgy

The Liturgy of the Word at Mass includes a Responsorial Psalm, which is divided into verses and responses.

Wisdom Literature

There are several books in the Old Testament that explore the meaning of life and give us practical advice for everyday living. Together these books are known as **Wisdom Literature.** These are the Wisdom books.

Job	one man's story that explores the meaning of suffering
Proverbs	short, poetic advice for everyday life
Ecclesiastes	a book that explores the meaning of human existence
Song of Songs	a love poem with many meanings
Wisdom of Solomon	poetic verses about justice and wisdom
Sirach	poetic verses about duty, humility, and the law

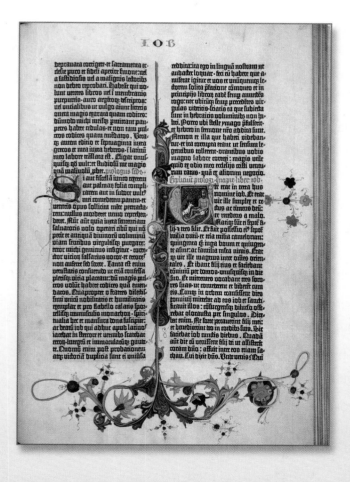

Why Wisdom?

Wisdom is one of the gifts of the Holy Spirit. Wisdom gives us understanding and helps us follow Jesus Christ. Through wisdom the Holy Spirit prepares us to recognize Christ and receive him as the Son of God and Savior of the world.

Mary, who trusted God with perfect obedience, is called the Seat of Wisdom. The Holy Spirit worked through Mary to prepare the world for the birth of Jesus. Mary had the wisdom and faith to cooperate with God and give birth to our Savior.

GO TO PAGE 240

Pray a Psalm

The psalms give us a way to pray about many aspects of life. When we are happy and full of hope, we can pray psalms of praise and thanksgiving. When we feel abandoned or sad, we can pray psalms asking God to be with us. When we have lost our way, we can pray psalms that lead us toward the light of God's promise. Pray this psalm together. Group A and Group B may read alternate verses.

Group A: The LORD answer you in time of distress;
the name of the God of Jacob defend you!

Group B: May God send you help from the temple,
from Zion be your support.

Group A: May God remember your every offering,
graciously accept your holocaust.

Group B: Grant what is in your heart,
fulfill your every plan.

All: May we shout for joy at your victory,
raise the banners in the name of our God.
The Lord grant your every prayer!

Group A: Now I know victory is given
to the anointed of the LORD.

Group B: God will answer him from the holy heavens
with a strong arm that brings victory.

Group A: Some rely on chariots, others on horses,
but we on the name of the LORD our God.

Group B: They collapse and fall,
but we stand strong and firm.

All: LORD, grant victory to the king;
answer when we call upon you.

Psalm 20

The Mission of the Church

Think of an activity in your church that proclaims Jesus' presence. Share it with others.

Prayer

Call me, Jesus, to act as a member of your Church. Help me to make you present to everyone I meet.

The Church Leads in Faith

After the Holy Spirit appeared to Peter and the apostles, they formed the early Church. Today the Church is still the sign and instrument of God's communion with all humanity. The Church unites people from around the world. We do not have to travel alone on our journey to God. The Church as the People of God goes ahead of us, teaching the truth and communicating faith.

God established the Church as the means of Salvation for all. God calls us to be members of the Church. Through Jesus Christ in the Church, we receive forgiveness from our sins and become part of God's family. As members of the Church, the Holy Spirit enables us to believe in Christ and to live as signs of God's presence in the world. When we celebrate the sacraments, practice our faith, and do good works, we act as members of God's family.

On Your Journey of Faith

Why is it important not to be alone on your journey of faith?

_____

_____

How do you show that you are a sign of God's presence in the world?

_____

_____

God and His People

In the Garden of Eden, God was present with Adam and Eve, and they walked and talked with him. Ever since their disobedience and exile from the garden, God has been bringing us back to a personal relationship with him.

▶ Noah's family stayed faithful to God even when no one else did.

▶ Abraham and his tribe became God's people, the Hebrews, who were God's presence among all other peoples of the world.

▶ David established rule over the people as king and God's representative.

▶ Solomon built the Temple, in which God could be present and be worshiped.

▶ Jesus came as God's presence among us. He demonstrated what God is like through his life, miracles, and teachings.

▶ Jesus Christ returned to the Father and established the Church to be God's presence on earth.

The People of God are all temples of the Holy Spirit. We carry God's presence in our hearts. We are also God's own family. We can talk with God and listen to him through prayer and the sacraments.

Reading God's Word

Just so, your light must shine before others, that they may see your good deeds and glorify your heavenly Father.

Matthew 5:16

GO TO PAGE 241

Praying the Lord's Prayer

The Lord's Prayer, which Jesus taught us, is one of our most important prayers. As you pray it, think about the deeper meaning of the words.

Our Father, who art in heaven,

How wonderful that I can call you Father, because you have created me. I am your child, but you are "our" Father. You are in heaven, but you are still with me. You share your life with me and are close to my heart.

hallowed be thy name; thy kingdom come, thy will be done on earth as it is in heaven.

Your name is holy, and you make all creation holy, including me. Keep me on the path to holiness. I pray for your kingdom to come. Thank you for bringing it near in your Son, Jesus Christ. Help me to serve your kingdom in the way I care for others.

Give us this day our daily bread,

You have given me life. How could you not give me the bread that I need? Help me to remember that it is "our" bread, one loaf that I must share with many.

and forgive us our trespasses, as we forgive those who trespass against us,

How can I ask for forgiveness if I am not willing to forgive? There is no limit to your forgiveness. May there be no limit to mine.

and lead us not into temptation, but deliver us from evil.

Give me the strength to face the daily struggles to make good choices. May the Holy Spirit help me to grow and give me peace.

Amen.

The Church Respects Other Religions

Jesus Christ, through his grace, can still save people who are not members of the Church. Jews responded to God's revelation in the Old Testament. Muslims—followers of Islam—believe in the one God of Abraham and his descendants. As Catholics we recognize and respect the value of other religions.

Images of the Church

Many images are used to describe the Church. Among them are the images of the Church as the Bride of Christ, the Temple of the Holy Spirit, and the Body of Christ.

Think of another image you could use to describe the Church. Complete the sentence below. Then draw a picture of your image.

The Church is like _____

_____

because _____

_____.

Faith Summary

Jesus Christ calls us to be members of the Church—the sign of God's communion with humanity. The mission of the Church is to proclaim Christ's presence today.

Word I Learned

crucified*

Ways of Being Like Jesus

Jesus taught us not to discriminate against other people. *Respect people of other religions.*

Prayer

Jesus, thank you for including me in your family, the Church, and for helping me be a sign of your presence in the world.

With My Family

Activity Assign each person a different family "body" part. Have the "mouth" of the family lead prayers, the "hands" help out with chores, and the "eyes" read from the Bible. At the end of the week, discuss how all the parts work together just like the Body of Christ.

Faith on the Go Ask one another: *How can we work as a family to be the Church to others?*

Family Prayer *Father God, teach us to be faithful members of the Body of Christ. Amen.*

* This word is taught with the Art Print. See page 241.

Marks of the Church

If someone asked you to explain the purpose of the Church, what would you say? Share what the Church means for you and your family.

Prayer

Jesus, lead me to love your Church so that I can be an important part of bringing your message to the world.

Marks of the Church

The **Nicene Creed** was written centuries ago to help Christians remember the important beliefs of the faith. In the Nicene Creed, we identify the four Marks of the Church. The four Marks of the Church are not characteristics that the Church creates, develops, or learns. They are qualities that Jesus Christ shares with his Church through the Holy Spirit. The four Marks of the Church are that it is one, holy, catholic, and apostolic.

The Church Is One

God is one in the Father, Son, and Holy Spirit. The Church is also one. Jesus Christ is the founder of the Church. Jesus brought us back to God and made us into the family of God. The Church is one in the Holy Spirit, and the Spirit dwells in those who believe.

The Church Is Holy

The Church is holy because the Church lives in union with Jesus Christ—the source of holiness. The Church leads others to holiness through the Holy Spirit. People can see the holiness of the Church in the love that Church members have for one another and in the many sacrifices they make for the sake of the world.

Link to Liturgy

At Sunday Mass after the Scripture readings and the Homily, we proclaim the Nicene Creed. The Creed is a summary of our Catholic faith. We stand to profess our faith before the world.

The Church Is Catholic

Catholic means "universal." The Church is universal in two ways. First, the Church is universal because all baptized people are part of the Church and possess the means of salvation. Second, the mission of the Church is universal because the Church is sent to proclaim Christ to the entire human race.

The Church Is Apostolic

The Church is apostolic because it traces its tradition directly from the apostles. With the Holy Spirit, the Church preserves and continues the teaching of the apostles. The pope and bishops are the successors of the apostles.

Mary, the Example of Perfect Holiness

Faithful Christians reflect the holiness of God. Mary is the greatest example of holiness. Mary goes before us in the holiness that is the mystery of the Church. Her song of response to God, titled the Magnificat, is in Luke 1:46–55. In that song Mary praises God for the gift of grace.

Reading God's Word

The Mighty One has done great things for me,
  and holy is his name.

Luke 1:49

GO TO PAGE 242

Praying the Nicene Creed

Below are verses from the Nicene Creed followed by passages to help you reflect on the prayer. These will help you talk with God the Father, Jesus the Son, and the Holy Spirit and to think about what the Creed means to you.

I believe in one God,
the Father almighty,
maker of heaven and earth,
of all things visible and invisible,

> Creator God, you are maker of heaven and earth. Your care continues for all of creation. You care for me; you are the Almighty, but you are also my loving Father.

I believe in one Lord Jesus Christ,
the Only Begotten Son of God,
born of the Father before all ages.
God from God, Light from Light,
true God from true God,

> Lord Jesus, how wonderful you are. You are God, but you are human, just like me. You are light, yet you know what it is like to be me. God and human together, you saved me.

I believe in the Holy Spirit, the Lord, the giver of life,
who proceeds from the Father and the Son,

> Holy Spirit, you give us life through the sacraments. You show me Christ, the visible image of God, and bring me into the love of the Trinity.

I believe in one, holy, catholic and apostolic Church.

> May our Church always be one. Keep the Church holy and lead me on the path to holiness.

and I look forward to the resurrection of the dead
and the life of the world to come.

> May I be united some day with all who have died to live in your presence forever.

Amen.

Peace and Unity

The peace we experience as God's people comes from our confidence in Jesus Christ and in the Church that he established. We can be at peace because our teachers and leaders have a clear understanding of what Jesus and the apostles taught. Therefore, we can learn from them and continue to grow closer to Christ. Many different people and cultures make up the Church, but this diversity does not affect the unity of the Church. God gives each of us different gifts, or virtues, to perform good works. We remain united because we worship the same God and receive help and grace from the same Savior, Jesus Christ.

Exploring Virtues

Explain how each of the following virtues helps us to celebrate the unity and diversity of the Church.

Humility _____

_____

Gentleness _____

_____

Patience _____

_____

Love _____

_____

Living My Faith

Faith Summary

The four Marks of the Church—that it is one, holy, catholic, and apostolic—are symbols of the Church's authority and mission. Through the unity of the Church, we can continue to grow closer to Christ and follow his example of love.

Words I Learned

Nicene Creed

Ways of Being Like Jesus

Jesus said the one characteristic that would set God's people apart and show the world God's presence is love. *Treat others with love and kindness.*

Prayer

Jesus, my friend, thank you for creating a Church that shares in your holiness and love. Help me to love the Church and the Church's leaders.

With My Family

Activity After Sunday Mass look through your parish bulletin with your family and list all the things your parish is doing to show that the Church is one, holy, catholic, and apostolic.

Faith on the Go Ask one another: *If someone asked what you do to live out the Marks of the Church, what would you say?*

Family Prayer Dear Jesus, grant our family the virtues we need to share your love and presence with those around us.

Celebrating Christmas

You may think of Christmas as a one-day celebration of Jesus' birth, but Christmas is actually a season of the liturgical year between Advent and Ordinary Time. The Christmas season begins on December 24 and continues for two or three weeks. During this time we welcome Jesus and celebrate other feasts, including the Feast of the Epiphany 12 days after Christmas. The season ends with the Feast of the Baptism of the Lord on the first Sunday after Epiphany. While Christmas is one of the shortest seasons, it is also one of the most joyful and exciting seasons.

The word *Christmas* comes from the Old English *Cristes Maesse*, meaning "Mass of Christ." Today we call it *Christmas* because we celebrate the birth of Christ at Mass. The Christmas season brings a joyful end to the Advent season, the four weeks when we prepare for and await the coming of Jesus.

Prayer

Dear Jesus, I am so happy to celebrate your birth! Please be with me as I learn more about the season of Christmas.

We Celebrate Epiphany During Christmas

Christmas is a season of holidays and feasts honoring Jesus and his family. One of the feasts we celebrate is **Epiphany.** The word *epiphany* means "revelation"— making something known. Epiphany celebrates the news of the birth of God's Son, Jesus, to the world. Three Magi were the first to proclaim Jesus as King.

At the time of Jesus' birth, a star appeared in the sky over Bethlehem where Jesus was born. The Magi from the East saw this star and set out in search of the newborn king to honor him with valuable gifts. During the journey the Magi stopped in Jerusalem to ask about the newborn king. King Herod, the leader of the Jewish people, secretly summoned the Magi. Fearing he might lose his power to this new king, Herod plotted to kill him. He told the Magi to return to Jerusalem once they found the new king so that he might visit and honor him as well.

When the Magi found the child in Bethlehem, they fell to their knees and offered their gifts to honor him. Later, in a dream, the Magi were warned not to return to King Herod and so left for their own country by another route. Their long and dangerous journey to honor the infant Jesus is the first acknowledgment that the Savior had been born.

adapted from Matthew 2:1–12

What are some ways you can honor Jesus in your life?_____

_____

How can you be like the shining star that guided the way to Jesus?_____

_____

Reading God's Word

They were overjoyed at seeing the star, and on entering the house they saw the child with Mary his mother. They prostrated themselves and did him homage.

Matthew 2:10–11

Mass During Christmas

During the Christmas season, the church is filled with a sense of excitement, festive decorations, and sounds of joyful carols. We hear readings about the birth of Jesus, the Holy Family, and Epiphany.

What We Experience

When you look around your church at Christmas, you will notice that the priest's vestments and the altar linens are bright white—the season's liturgical color. You will see a nativity scene with the infant Jesus. You may also see images of three camels and Caspar, Melchior, and Balthazar, traditional names of the Magi who were guided by the star to Bethlehem.

Jesus and the Magi

Epiphany is the revelation of Jesus as the Son of God. While Mary and Joseph knew he was the Son of God, no one else was aware. Led by a star, the Magi arrived with gifts to honor the newborn king. The arrival of the Magi acknowledges to the world that the Son of God, Jesus, has been born.

Gifts of the Magi

Use the code to figure out the gifts the Magi brought to honor Jesus. Then check your answers by reading Matthew 2:11 in your Bible.

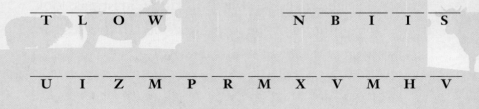

T	L	O	W			N	B	I	I	S

U	I	Z	M	P	R	M	X	V	M	H	V

KEY

A=Z
B=Y
C=X
D=W
E=V
F=U
G=T
H=S
I=R
J=Q
K=P
L=O
M=N
N=M
O=L
P=K
Q=J
R=I
S=H
T=G
U=F
V=E
W=D
X=C
Y=B
Z=A

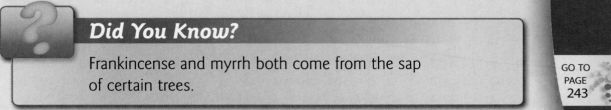

Did You Know?

Frankincense and myrrh both come from the sap of certain trees.

GO TO PAGE 243

Living My Faith

Faith Summary

Christmas is more than just December 25, the day we celebrate Jesus' birthday. It is a season of the liturgical year when we celebrate several feasts, including the Feast of the Epiphany. On that day we celebrate the visit of the Magi to the infant Jesus, the day that Jesus was revealed as the Savior of the world.

Word I Learned

Epiphany

Ways of Being Like Jesus

Jesus spent much time with his followers. *Take part in parish activities such as food drives and social events.*

Prayer

Dear God, thank you for the gift of your Son, Jesus! Help me, by my example, show others the way Jesus wants us to live.

With My Family

Activity When you go to church during Christmas, look around for examples of the ideas described in this session. Discuss what you see with your family.

Faith on the Go Ask one another: *What is one thing you can do to be a "shining star" for Jesus?*

Family Prayer Use Christmas as a time to pray and ask for God's help to turn every worry that drifts into your thoughts to a prayer for peace.

Sacraments, Our Way of Life

Saint Ignatius of Loyola

As the leader of the Society of Jesus, Saint Ignatius found strength in his deep prayer life and his love for the Mass.

Saint Ignatius of Loyola

In 1540 Ignatius and six of his companions formed a religious community known as the Society of Jesus, or the Jesuits. The new community elected Ignatius as their leader. The Society of Jesus expanded very quickly throughout Europe and as far away as Japan, where Ignatius's dear friend Francis Xavier proclaimed the Gospel as a missionary.

Ignatius could not have kept up the great work that he did without a deep prayer life. The center of Ignatius's prayer life was the celebration of Mass. Before he celebrated Mass, Ignatius took two hours to prepare and reflect on the experience of encountering Jesus in the Mass. Ignatius ordered his followers not to disturb him during this time. He loved to celebrate Masses that honored the Blessed Trinity, the Holy Name of Jesus, and Mary, the Mother of God. During Mass Ignatius prayed for himself, the Jesuit community, and all the people whom they served. Ignatius had his deepest experiences of God during these times of prayer. These experiences of prayer and devotion gave him the grace to face the issues in his life and of the Jesuit ministry. His feast day is July 31.

Saint Ignatius founded the Roman College of the Jesuits in Italy.

Some friends will tell us what we want to hear, but our best friends will tell us the truth and help us grow. Who are the people in your life whom you can count on to help you live according to your faith?

Prophets Challenge the People

Prayer

Dear God, open my mind and heart to hear the truth of your message.

The Prophets

After King Solomon's reign, his kingdom was divided into two smaller kingdoms—Israel to the north and Judah to the south. During this time God called on certain people to be **prophets.** Each prophet proclaimed a message that responded to his own particular time and situation.

Prophets held a unique role in ancient Jewish society because they spoke for God. For the most part, the prophets advised people, especially kings, about how their societies could exist in harmony with God's commandments. Both kingdoms, Israel and Judah, had their own problems. Because of this, God gave them their own prophets to overcome these issues.

Amos and Jeremiah

Between 760 and 750 B.C., the prophet Amos spoke out against the way in which the wealthy people of the northern kingdom were treating those who were poor. Amos's concern for justice is part of the basis for the Church's teachings about justice today. The prophet Jeremiah spent a lifetime in the southern kingdom, sharing God's message with the people of Judah. He harshly criticized the rulers, the priests, and the people for not obeying the terms of the covenant established with Abraham and Moses. When the Babylonian empire conquered Judah in 587 B.C., Jeremiah witnessed the destruction of Solomon's Temple in Jerusalem. This was one of the saddest events in Jewish history. It marked the beginning of the Babylonian exile. Thousands of Jews were forced to leave Judah and settle in Babylon. Jeremiah's advice encouraged the exiles. He urged them to remember that God loved them no matter where they were.

God Calls Isaiah

Sometimes God calls someone to be a prophet in a spectacular way. One such calling came to a man named Isaiah, who prophesied in Jerusalem before the time of Jeremiah.

Isaiah was in the Temple of Jerusalem when he had a sudden, powerful vision of God sitting on an enormous throne, wearing clothes that flowed across the room. Six-winged angel guardians, called **seraphim,** hovered above, crying, "Holy, holy, holy is the Lord of hosts!" The entire Temple shook and filled with smoke.

This certainly got Isaiah's attention. He responded, "I am a man of unclean lips, living among a people of unclean lips." Isaiah felt that he was not worthy to be in God's presence. One of the seraphim responded by taking an ember from the live coals on the altar and touching Isaiah's mouth with it. The angel said, "See, now that this has touched your lips, your wickedness is removed, your sin purged."

Then Isaiah heard God's voice saying, "Whom shall I send? Who will go for us?" Isaiah, now free from feeling unworthy to be in God's company, said, "Here I am; send me!"

adapted from Isaiah 6:1–8

The man who had felt unworthy just moments earlier was now ready to do God's work.

Seraphim taking an ember from the live coals on the altar to clean Isaiah's mouth

Reading God's Word

Comfort, give comfort to my people, says your God.

Isaiah 40:1

GO TO
PAGE
244

Send Me, Lord

Prophets have always helped us relate the issues of the present to God's everlasting message. With this prayer you can ask God to help you hear people who are like prophets and to be more like a prophet for others.

Holy God,
help me to listen with my heart
when you tell me the truth about my life.
Help me to agree when you show me my sin
and help me to hope when you show me
how to change.
Help me to live out your truth in my own life
and to encourage others to do the same.
Thank you for speaking to my heart,
helping me to feel your love and concern.
Thank you for using my mind, voice, and body
to carry out your ministry in the world.
In the name of Jesus,
my prophet, priest, and king.
Amen.

Now take time to thank God for sending prophets to help us live out God's truth in our lives. Think about one thing God might be asking you to change in your life. Ask God to help you make that change and live as he calls you to live. Thank him for the grace and guidance of the Holy Spirit in your life.

What It Means to Reform

Some of the kings in the history of Israel and Judah did their best to bring **reform,** or change, to their societies. With the help of the prophets, these kings called their people to turn from their evil ways, honor God, and treat one another—especially those who are poor and weak— with respect. Reform continues to be an important part of society today. People are still trying to make positive changes in governments, communities, and schools. One of the reasons people work for reform is that the laws of society are not always the same as the moral laws required by faith. As Catholics we follow the moral laws of our faith, even when they do not agree with the laws of society.

Work for Reform

If God called upon you today to be a prophet for reform, what do you think he would want you to work on? Why?

_____

_____

_____

Meet a Modern Prophet

Dorothy Day (1897–1980) cofounded the Catholic Worker Movement, a community of laypeople that serves those in need. Day was a passionate advocate for peace. She was arrested several times for protesting the United States' involvement in war. Some consider Dorothy Day a modern-day prophet. In 2000 the archbishop of New York formally asked the pope to consider declaring Dorothy Day a saint.

Living My Faith

Faith Summary

God's prophets were called to remind people of God's message. Sometimes they pointed out the consequences of people's sinful lives, and sometimes they brought encouragement during hard times.

Words I Learned

prophets   **reform**   **seraphim**

Ways of Being Like Jesus

As a prophet, Jesus was aware of the injustices in society and called on people to reform. *Speak out against the injustices in your society and work for reform.*

Prayer

Holy God, thank you for sending your prophets to tell us what we need to hear. Help me be more open to listening to the people in my life who are honest with me and encourage me.

With My Family

Activity Find a magazine article about a social injustice. With the help of your family, write a letter to the editor of that magazine in response to the article.

Faith on the Go Ask one another: *What is our family being called to do to help others? How can we respond to that call?*

Family Prayer *Heavenly Father, help each of us respond, "Here I am, Lord! Send me!" whenever and wherever you call us to serve. Amen.*

Have you ever gone somewhere you did not want to go? Maybe you had to move to a new town or start at a new school. How did you make the best of your situation?

Prophets Give Hope

Prayer

Lord Jesus, help me to hear the message of the prophets so that I can better know the story of my Christian faith.

The Jews in Exile

During the Babylonian exile, when the Jewish people of Judah were forced to settle in Babylon, they did not know when or if they would ever return home to Jerusalem. Their great city and the Temple had been destroyed, and they were captives living in the land of their enemies. They were severely mistreated, and they mourned for the people who had been killed during the war. They saw no end to their misery.

It was during this time that a new prophet began ministering to the exiled Jews. He admired Isaiah and even took the same name, although today we call him Second Isaiah. The prophet proclaimed to the people that God still loved them and would care for them, even during this difficult time in an unfriendly place. Second Isaiah emphasized that God would continue to act for his people, as he had done in the past. He wanted them to know that God, who had led their ancestors out of Egypt, would lead them on another exodus back to the **Promised Land**—the land God had given to his people.

The Holy Spirit called on Second Isaiah to comfort the exiles. There was good reason for the prophet to speak encouraging words. The period of exile (587–537 B.C.) had been bitter. The people dreamed of returning to Jerusalem. As time went on, memories of their homeland faded more and more.

Early Christians Turn to the Prophecies

The Gospel writers used the Old Testament to help them understand Jesus and his message. The writers found the teachings of Second Isaiah to be the most helpful. They wrote that Second Isaiah's message of renewal and hope was ultimately fulfilled in the life, Death, and Resurrection of Jesus Christ. Luke, for example, refers to Isaiah 40:3–5 as he tells the story of John the Baptist's ministry and his promise that Jesus the Messiah would come (Luke 3:4–6).

Of course, the Jewish exiles understood Second Isaiah's message to mean that God would save them and that they would return home to Jerusalem. Early Christians, however, believed that the messages of Second Isaiah and other prophets referred to Jesus, who would save all people, not just the Jewish exiles.

John the Baptist was a prophet who spoke of the coming of Jesus the Messiah.

Reading God's Word

A voice cries out: In the desert prepare the way of the LORD!

Isaiah 40:3

GO TO PAGE 245

Pray a Psalm

The following prayer is from the first part of Psalm 143.
It is a call to God for strength during difficult times.

Group A: *Lord, hear my prayer;*
in your faithfulness listen to my pleading;
answer me in your justice.

Group B: *Do not enter into judgment with your servant;*
before you no living being can be just.

All: *I stretch out my hands to you;*
I thirst for you like a parched land.

Group A: *The enemy has pursued me;*
they have crushed my life to the ground.

Group B: *They have left me in darkness*
like those long dead.

All: *I stretch out my hands to you;*
I thirst for you like a parched land.

Group A: *My spirit is faint within me;*
my heart is dismayed.

Group B: *I remember the days of old;*
I ponder all your deeds;
the works of your hands I recall.

All: *I stretch out my hands to you;*
I thirst for you like a parched land.

Be aware of God's love and strength surrounding you.
Ask God for what you most need right now. Thank him
for his love and presence. Rest peacefully in God for a
few moments.

2ND ISAIAH

Comfort, give comfort to my people,
says your GOD.
Speak tenderly to Jerusalem, and proclaim to her
that her service is at an end,
her guilt is expiated (IS 40:1-2)

Connecting Matthew and Isaiah

Early Christians, especially the Gospel writers, found the teaching of Second Isaiah to be helpful in understanding Jesus' message. They also believed that Isaiah's messages referred to the coming of Jesus. Complete the activity below to see how Matthew connected Jesus' story to the prophets of the past. Determine the passage from the Book of Isaiah that Matthew used to tell the story of Jesus. Then describe the event to which each passage refers. Choose from the following passages from Isaiah: 7:14; 40:3; 50:6; 53:4; 53:7.

New Testament	Old Testament	The Event
Matthew 1:23	Isaiah _____ : _____	
Matthew 3:3	Isaiah _____ : _____	
Matthew 8:17	Isaiah _____ : _____	
Matthew 26:63	Isaiah _____ : _____	
Matthew 27:30	Isaiah _____ : _____	

Faith Summary

Second Isaiah prophesied during the Babylonian exile. His message to the exiled Jews was to remain hopeful by remembering God's promise. Early Christians believed Second Isaiah had foretold the coming of Jesus.

Words I Learned

Promised Land

Ways of Being Like Jesus

Isaiah and the prophets offered hope during difficult times. All our hope is fulfilled in Jesus Christ. *Offer hope to those who need it.*

Prayer

Thank you, Jesus, for fulfilling what all the other prophets and priests and kings began. I no longer have to hope for some distant savior—you are with me now.

With My Family

Activity Think of a friend or a relative whom your family has not been in touch with recently. Write that person a card or send a small gift to remind that person that your family is thinking about him or her.

Faith on the Go Ask one another: *In what ways can we offer hope to those in need?*

Family Prayer *Almighty God, help us remember to turn to you always, especially when we are in need of comfort and hope. Amen.*

Sacraments of Initiation

Think of several important events that have impacted your life. How have these events changed you? How did you react to each event?

Prayer

Lord Jesus, call me to live as a member of your family so that I can enjoy the strength that comes from you and your people.

Entering a New Life with God's Family

We enter a new life with Christ and become members of the Church through the Sacraments of Initiation. These sacraments are Baptism, the Eucharist, and Confirmation.

Parents have their babies baptized not long after they are born. Parents know that Baptism is necessary for Salvation. Baptism marks the baby as a member of the Church. The community of believers makes a commitment to care for and teach the child as he or she grows up in the faith.

In the early Church, people who wanted to become members of God's family traditionally were adults. They had to go through a long conversion period. This type of preparation for adult Baptism still exists. Adults who are going through this process are called **catechumens.** During this time of preparation, catechumens learn about what God has done through Jesus, what the Church teaches, and how to respond to God's call.

Importance of Water in Scripture

The Old Testament uses many images of water that can help us understand Baptism. Each year during the **Easter Vigil,** the baptismal waters are blessed, and the prayers we pray call to mind the images of water. What Bible stories can you think of that involve water? On a separate sheet of paper, illustrate the Bible story.

_____

_____

_____

Link to Liturgy

We bless ourselves with holy water as we enter church as a reminder of our Baptism.

The Eucharist

You probably remember receiving your First Holy Communion. It was a special day that you celebrated with your whole family. It may have included a special meal with your family after Mass. At Mass the parish welcomed you and the others who received their First Holy Communion and joined with you in receiving the Eucharist.

Every time the Eucharist is celebrated, we remember the sacrifice that Jesus made for us and for our Salvation. On the night before he died, he blessed the bread and gave it to his disciples saying, "This is my Body." Then he blessed the wine, distributed it and said, "This is my Blood." Each time Mass is celebrated and the priest repeats these words of consecration, the bread and wine become the Body and Blood of Jesus Christ. When we receive Holy Communion, Jesus Christ becomes food for our journey.

There was a time when people would receive the Eucharist only once or twice a year. Today the Church encourages us to receive the Eucharist every time we attend Mass, especially on Sundays or Holy Days of Obligation. Many Catholics take advantage of the celebration of the Eucharist in their parishes and receive Holy Communion every day. In this way they prepare themselves to share God's love with all people they meet that day.

Reading God's Word

Jesus said to them, "Amen, amen, I say to you, unless you eat the flesh of the Son of Man and drink his blood, you do not have life within you. Whoever eats my flesh and drinks my blood has eternal life, and I will raise him on the last day."

John 6:53–54

GO TO PAGE 246

Growing in Christ

When you face a new situation, it may help teach you a new lesson. Even though you have been growing in faith since you were a baby, there will always be more to learn about life in God's family.

Saint Richard of Chichester, who lived during the 13th century, wrote the prayer on which this prayer is based. The prayer reminds us of the day-by-day growth we experience as Christians.

> *Thanks be to you, our Lord Jesus Christ,*
> *For all the benefits that you have given us,*
> *For all the pains and insults that you have borne for us.*
> *Most merciful Redeemer, Friend, and Brother,*
> *May we know you more clearly,*
> *Love you more dearly,*
> *And follow you more nearly,*
> *Day by day.*
> *Amen.*

You have been marked for life. Spend some quiet time now with Jesus. Thank him for the day-to-day growth you have experienced since your Baptism. Ask him for the help you need to follow his ways and grow in your love for him.

Changed for Life

Some experiences can change the way we look at life. The Sacraments of Initiation change us spiritually. Through Baptism we receive Salvation and a permanent mark, or character. We experience Baptism only once, but we belong to Christ forever. We receive the gift of sanctifying grace. The Eucharist brings us closer to God and our Catholic community. It nourishes and strengthens us.

Confirmation deepens our faith. The Spirit imparts wisdom so that we can live as God wants us to live. Confirmation deepens our bond with the Church. The Holy Spirit gives us strength to know Christ and live like him. We receive the grace to become more active in our faith.

At Confirmation we are anointed on the forehead with Chrism—special oil blessed for this purpose. The bishop lays hands on us and says, "Be sealed with the Gift of the Holy Spirit." Like Baptism, Confirmation leaves a permanent spiritual mark and therefore cannot be repeated.

Changed Lives Are Meant to Change Lives

Just as Jesus' baptism marked the beginning of his ministry, our Baptism obligates us to do God's work. As we live filled with faith and love, we show others what a fulfilling life truly is. We demonstrate love, forgiveness, and hope because we personally know these things from our relationship with God through Jesus Christ and the Holy Spirit.

Turning Points

Baptism, First Holy Communion, and Confirmation are important events in people's lives. What do these ceremonies mean to you?

_____

_____

_____

On a separate sheet of paper, draw symbols for each Sacrament of Initiation.

Living My Faith

Faith Summary

Baptism, the Eucharist, and Confirmation are Sacraments of Initiation. Each of these sacraments brings us closer to Christ and to our own Catholic community.

Words I Learned

catechumens

Easter Vigil

Ways of Being Like Jesus

Jesus' public ministry began after John baptized him. *Act as a forgiving and caring member of the Christian community.*

Prayer

Jesus, thank you for accepting me into your family. As a member of your family, I know there will always be someone to love me, and there will always be other people for me to love.

With My Family

Activity Make a family scrapbook of celebrations for the Sacraments of Initiation. Include pictures and descriptions.

Faith on the Go Ask one another: *How does your faith give you a firm foundation for living?*

Family Prayer *Come Holy Spirit, renew us and strengthen us through the sacraments so that we can show hope and love and learn to forgive.*

Sacraments of Healing

Recall a time when you were very sick. How did the sickness change your daily life? Who helped you to recover? How did you thank that person?

Prayer

Jesus, my guide, help me always to know that you are ready to offer me healing in body and spirit.

Healing for the Body

The Church continues Jesus' healing ministry with the Sacrament of the Anointing of the Sick. When a person is seriously ill, is preparing for surgery, is of advanced age, or is in danger of death, he or she may celebrate the Anointing of the Sick with a priest. The priest anoints the person with the oil of the sick—olive oil that has been blessed by a bishop. This sacrament

Little Girl Arise, Laura James, acrylic on canvas.

▶ helps a sick person identify his or her physical suffering more closely with Christ's.

▶ gives strength, peace, and courage to a person who is dealing with serious illness or the difficulties of aging.

▶ forgives the sins of a person who is unable to participate in the Sacrament of Penance and Reconciliation.

▶ may even bring physical healing if that is God's will.

▶ helps to prepare a believer for eternal life.

The Dignity of Human Life

The Church teaches that human life is sacred because it comes from God. When people are seriously ill, they should be treated with dignity because God created them. Christ's healing power is with us at all times, no matter how bad a situation may look. The Church condemns the practice of **euthanasia** because life is sacred. It is not acceptable to end a person's life just because that person is old or seriously ill.

Link to Liturgy

During Holy Week the bishop celebrates the Chrism Mass with the priests of the diocese. At this Mass the bishop consecrates and distributes Chrism that will be used in Baptisms, Confirmations, and Holy Orders. He also blesses the oil of the catechumens and the oil of the sick.

Healing for the Soul

In the Sacrament of Penance and Reconciliation, the Holy Spirit gives us the grace of healing from serious sin and the effects of sin. All sin separates us from God and others. Mortal sin especially separates us from God, and someone who does not repent may be in danger of hell—the eternal punishment of separation from God. All mortal sins must be confessed in the Sacrament of Reconciliation.

We celebrate the Sacrament of Reconciliation after a careful examination of conscience. In the sacrament a person makes a confession to a priest, who offers absolution, conveying God's forgiveness of the sins confessed. The Catholic tradition offers us some general steps for making a good confession:

1. Make a thoughtful and honest examination of conscience.
2. Express true sorrow for the sins committed.
3. Make a firm commitment to change.
4. Confess those sins to the priest.
5. Receive absolution.
6. Perform the penance given by the priest.

Reconciliation helps us reunite with God and the Church. It eases our consciences, brings us peace, and comforts us spiritually.

At the time of death, some people who are saved are not yet ready to be in God's presence. These souls rest in Purgatory, which is the temporary state of final preparation and purification. The prayers of other Christians help those in Purgatory to attain full union with God.

GO TO PAGE 247

A Call for Mercy

We all know what it is like to feel sad or guilty after doing something we know is wrong. We call on God's mercy and forgiveness with this prayer.

Act of Contrition

My God,
I am sorry for my sins with all my heart.
In choosing to do wrong
and failing to do good,
I have sinned against you
whom I should love above all things.
I firmly intend, with your help,
to do penance,
to sin no more,
and to avoid whatever leads me to sin.
Our Savior Jesus Christ
suffered and died for us.
In his name, my God, have mercy.

Now spend some time with God. Ask him for the help you need to avoid what leads to sin and for the strength to ask forgiveness when you have done something wrong. Thank him in your own words for the forgiveness he offers.

Removing the Effects of Sin

When a person is forgiven for stealing something, he or she must still give back or pay for whatever was stolen. The effects of sin can remain in a person's life even after the sins are forgiven. After receiving absolution, a person must also give restitution by making up for the harm that was done to the victim.

After experiencing forgiveness a person may feel inclined to commit a particular sin again because the temptation is still there in that person's life. A penance of prayers and good deeds may help a person to overcome these temptations. Through prayers and good deeds, we can receive indulgences. The practice of praying for and receiving indulgences can help us grow closer to God and others.

Giving Restitution

Imagine that you stole something without anyone finding out. You still feel guilty about what you did. What can you do to make restitution for your sin?

_____

_____

_____

Imagine that you insulted someone and feel guilty about what you said. How can you make up for what you said?

_____

_____

_____

Faith Summary

In celebrating the Sacraments of Healing, we can experience the healing presence of God in our everyday lives. Restitution, penance, and indulgences are ways to continue the reconciliation process even after confession and forgiveness.

Word I Learned

euthanasia

Ways of Being Like Jesus

Jesus included every person in his mission to heal physical and spiritual ailments. *Do not exclude anyone in activities at school, at home, in your parish, and in your community.*

Prayer

Jesus, thank you for healing me in every way. Help me turn to you when I need my body or my spirit to be healed.

With My Family

Activity Think about ways in which the world needs healing. Each day this week, write one global problem on a sheet of paper and attach it to your refrigerator. With your family, pray for a solution before each meal.

Faith on the Go Ask one another: *What first step can you take to bring healing to your world?*

Family Prayer *Dear Jesus, we are sorry for the times we make bad choices and sin. Remind us to be kind and treat others as you would treat them. Amen.*

Celebrating Lent and Holy Week

Lent is the season in our Church's liturgical year when we remember Jesus' greatest sacrifice—his Crucifixion and Death on the cross. It is a time for prayer and reflection. We reflect on how we have been living, and we open our hearts and minds to accept God's gift of grace.

We celebrate Lent following the first part of Ordinary Time that follows the Christmas season. Lent begins in late winter on Ash Wednesday and ends in early- to mid-spring on the evening of Holy Thursday. On Ash Wednesday we receive ashes on our foreheads as a reminder of our sinfulness. We ask for God's forgiveness and show that we are sorry. During Holy Week and the Triduum, we remember Jesus' entrance into Jerusalem on Palm Sunday, the Last Supper on Holy Thursday, Jesus' Death on Good Friday, and his Resurrection at the Easter Vigil on Holy Saturday. As we remember Jesus' suffering and Death, we pray that we are ready to celebrate his Resurrection.

Prayer

Dear Jesus, thank you for walking by my side during this season of Lent. Help me be ready to assist those in need.

We Fast and Pray During Lent and Holy Week

Lent is a time of **fasting** and prayer. The Church asks that we fast during Lent by limiting or going without certain foods. We also give up meat every Friday and limit the size of our meals on Ash Wednesday and Good Friday. As we pay closer attention to fasting, we become more aware of the struggles that others face each day. Likewise, we are reminded of our total dependence on God and our spiritual hunger for his love and grace.

We pray to God during Lent and Holy Week and ask that through our fasting, we become more aware of others and show that we care by lending a helping hand wherever we can.

Some people eat hot-cross buns on Good Friday. The cross on the bun is a symbol for the Crucifixion.

How Can I Help?

Jesus asks that we share with others the love he shares with us. How can you show this love and lend a helping hand to those in need? Write three ways you can help below. Return to this page throughout Lent as a reminder of ways you can help those in need.

1. _____

   _____

2. _____

   _____

3. _____

   _____

Reading God's Word

You shall love your neighbor as yourself.   *Matthew 22:39*

Mass During Lent and Holy Week

During Lent we hear readings about the events that lead to Jesus' suffering and Death. The readings remind us that Lent is a time to reflect. We often realize we have not acted like Jesus would want us to. We are reminded that God will forgive us if we ask.

What We Experience

During Lent the church environment encourages reflection. The priest's vestments are purple. The sanctuary decorations are simple and understated. During Lent many people celebrate the Sacrament of Reconciliation, a source of healing and strength. Through reflection, prayer, and fasting, we see that we have sinned, but we learn that God is always ready to forgive us.

The Wonderful Gift of Reliance

Lent is a time to remember how much we rely on God. We pray and ask God to help us understand all that Jesus did for us. God gives us eternal life through the Death and Resurrection of his Son, Jesus. All that we do and all that we are happen because of God's great love. Take a moment to think about this wonderful gift. Fill in the stepping stones, telling about times that you rely on God.

Did You Know?

The fourth Sunday during Lent is sometimes called Laetare Sunday. This marks the halfway point of the season and is marked by rose vestments instead of violet.

GO TO PAGE 248

Living My Faith

Faith Summary

Lent is a time of fasting and prayer. We fast as a reminder of the needs of others and our own reliance on God. During Lent we also celebrate the Sacrament of Reconciliation. It is a source of healing and strength that helps prepare us to celebrate Easter.

Word I Learned

fasting

Ways of Being Like Jesus

Jesus asks that we love our enemies and treat them well. *Pray that you're able to forgive those who do you harm and show them kindness.*

Prayer

Dear God, help us to see others who need our help and understanding. Be our shining light and guide us to do all that's in our power to help and comfort them.

With My Family

Activity When you go to Mass during Lent and Holy Week, look around your church. Find examples of what you learned in this session. Discuss with your family what you see.

Faith on the Go Ask one another: *Where is one place you can go to during Lent to pray and prepare yourself to receive the Sacrament of Reconciliation?*

Family Prayer During Lent and Holy Week, invite family members to take turns praying for church leaders and your parish clergy.

Morality, Our Lived Faith

Saint Benedict of Palermo

Benedict was a former slave who became the leader of a community of monks in 1578. He was known for his humble manner and for the ability to give insightful advice.

Saint Benedict of Palermo

Benedict was born in Messina, Sicily, in 1526. His parents were slaves who had been brought to Sicily from Africa, so Benedict was also a slave. He gained his freedom at the age of 18. Benedict worked for his former master for several years after he was freed. While Benedict was working one day, a neighbor, Father Jerome Lanza, approached him. Father Lanza convinced him to follow Jesus. Benedict sold his possessions, gave the money to those who were poor, and joined the monastery.

At the monastery Benedict and others lived as hermits. They endured harsh conditions. They ate very little, did difficult manual labor, and knelt in prayer for hours on stone floors. Benedict felt that even this lifestyle was too comfortable. After making a pilgrimage to the deserts of Syria and Egypt, Benedict decided to leave Father Lanza's monastery.

Eventually Benedict retreated to a cave in the mountains overlooking Palermo, Sicily. It was during this time that people began to regard Benedict as an especially holy man. They came from near and far to see him and ask for his blessings. His reputation grew even greater after he joined the Convent of St. Mary. At the convent he was appointed the superior. Humble Benedict, however, did not want to be in a position of authority. After serving as superior for a short time, he resigned. He preferred to work in the kitchen as a cook.

Benedict died in 1589 and was declared a saint in 1807. He is a patron saint of African Americans, and his feast day is April 4.

When was the last time you chose to help someone rather than do something for yourself? What did you do to help? How did you feel afterward?

Jesus' Way of Love

Prayer

Jesus, help me choose to love even when it is difficult and help me live out my love in my relationships with you and others.

The Three Theological Virtues

God gives us the three Theological Virtues. We do not acquire them through human effort. The Theological Virtues are deeply connected to one another. We can hope because we have faith and, as Saint Paul writes in the First Letter to the Corinthians, we demonstrate our faith and hope through charity.

Faith

Faith is the ability to believe in God and to give our lives to him. Through the Church, the Holy Spirit shares with us the ability to believe. Faith calls us not only to believe in God but also to decide to give ourselves totally to him. When you give your life to God, you are acting for the good of others.

Faith

Hope

Christian hope is our desire for all the good things God has planned for us. Hope helps us trust that if we live according to Jesus' teachings, we will see God's kingdom. Hope also helps us do what pleases God, even when it is difficult or when we get discouraged. Through Christian hope we know that we have eternal life—our existence with God forever in Heaven. We often say offhandedly that we "hope" something will happen. This expression is more like a wish than Christian hope. Christian hope is based on the Bible and the teachings of the Church. Christian hope gives us confidence that God's plan will unfold, as it should—even if it doesn't happen right now or in the way we expect. The Holy Spirit gives us this kind of hope.

Hope

Charity

Charity

Charity is the virtue we use to show our love for God. This love is more than just feelings for God; it is the way we think and act toward him. When we love God, we allow him to be at the center of our lives. We ask for his help in everything we say and do. We also exhibit charity in our love for other people. We often use the word *charity* to mean "the giving away of money or possessions to those who are poor." Jesus taught us that sometimes we are also called to make sacrifices to show our love for all.

The practice of charity, or love, brings the three Theological Virtues together in perfect harmony. Saint Paul wrote about this in his letter to the Corinthians.

"If I have faith to move mountains but do not have love, I am nothing.
Love is patient and kind; love is not jealous or boastful.
Love believes all things, hopes all things, endures all things.
So faith, hope and love remain, these three. But the greatest of these is love."

adapted from 1 Corinthians 13:1–13

Living the Virtues

Imagine what the world would be like if we all lived with faith, hope, and charity. How do you think the world would be different?

_____

_____

_____

_____

GO TO PAGE 249

Praying the Virtues

Through prayer we strengthen our relationship with God and accept the gifts that the Holy Spirit grants us—faith, hope, and charity.

Act of Faith

O my God, I firmly believe that you are one God in three divine Persons, Father, Son, and Holy Spirit. I believe that your divine Son became man and died for our sins, and that he will come to judge the living and the dead. I believe these and all the truths which the holy Catholic Church teaches, because you have revealed them, who can neither deceive nor be deceived. Amen.

After you pray the Act of Faith, think about how God, Jesus, and the Holy Spirit influence your life. Ask God to strengthen your faith, give you hope, and encourage you to be charitable.

Living the Theological Virtues

Have you ever tried to pay close attention to God for an entire day? It's not easy to do. The ability to focus on God in this way is really a gift of the Holy Spirit. Saint Thérèse had such a gift. People wanted to know about how she did it, so she wrote her story and called it *The Story of a Soul*. People today still read and learn from her story.

Thérèse died at the young age of 24. She practiced faith, hope, and charity so well that she was **canonized**—declared a saint of the Church—in 1925. Saint Thérèse's feast day is October 1. Pope John Paul II declared her a **Doctor of the Church** in 1997. A Doctor of the Church is one who gives special guidance to Christians seeking a deeper spiritual life. There are two other female Doctors of the Church: Saint Catherine of Siena and Saint Teresa of Ávila. Although Thérèse's life was short, her story is an inspiring reminder that we can all live as members of God's kingdom. Our identity as members of the Kingdom of God is based on how we demonstrate the Theological Virtues through our actions.

Showing Faith, Hope, and Charity

Think about ways you show faith, hope, and charity in your own life. Write two examples for each of the Theological Virtues.

Faith	Hope	Charity

Faith Summary

The three Theological Virtues—faith, hope, and charity— are gifts from God. Faith calls us to make a personal decision to give our lives fully to God. Hope gives us the strength to live for the Kingdom of God and to accept the Holy Spirit in our lives. Charity is the virtue that guides our actions to love God and others.

Words I Learned

canonized   **Doctor of the Church**

Ways of Being Like Jesus

Jesus taught that the loving thing to do is sometimes the opposite of what we might want to do. *Think of a person with whom you have not been very friendly and do something nice for that person.*

Prayer

God, thank you for the gifts of faith, hope, and charity, which make me secure in you.

With My Family

Activity Develop a family motto based on the three Theological Virtues. Keep it short—one or two sentences—and then design it, and hang it up on a wall or on the refrigerator.

Faith on the Go Ask one another: *Think about your special gifts from God. How do you share these gifts with others?*

Family Prayer *Holy Spirit, thank you for all the gifts you have given us. Help us to live out the gifts of faith, hope, and charity every day.*

What do you think your life will be like in 20 years? What kind of job will you have? Will you have a family?

Sacraments of Service

Prayer

Jesus, help me trust that the decisions I make will lead me to a life filled with love and holiness. Make me holy, as you are holy.

Sacraments of Service

Both priesthood and marriage are vocations. A vocation is a way of life to which God calls us so that we can live out the mission of the Church. Through our vocations we use the gifts God has given us to love others and to serve the Kingdom of God.

The Holy Spirit calls people to holiness with the Sacraments of Holy Orders and Matrimony. Holy Orders and Matrimony are called the Sacraments at the Service of Communion. These sacraments are ways of life that help us to lead others to Salvation. We read in Leviticus 11:44, "For I, the LORD, am your God; and you shall make and keep yourselves holy, because I am holy."

Matrimony

Think about God's Covenant with Moses and the Hebrews. In the Sacrament of Matrimony, or marriage, a man and a woman enter into a covenant with God and each other. Marriage is an example of the relationship between Christ and his bride, the Church. The people in a marriage are called to serve each other, their family, and the church.

During the marriage ceremony, the man and the woman consent to the sacrament and state their promises to each other. The couple declare that they have come freely to give themselves to each other and to seal their love in the presence of the Church. The priest or deacon is a witness to the sacrament and blesses the couple. The priest or deacon blesses wedding rings and the couple exchange them as symbols of love and fidelity. The rings show others that the couple are committed to their marriage.

Serving God, the Church, and the World

The Holy Spirit calls men to a life of holiness and service as leaders of the Church in the Sacrament of Holy Orders. This sacrament gives priests the grace and spiritual power to perform sacraments. Through this sacrament the Holy Spirit imparts a special mark that changes a priest forever and identifies him as one of God's servants. A bishop places his hands on the head of the man to be ordained and says, "Hear us, Lord our God, and pour out upon these servants of yours the blessing of the Holy Spirit and the grace and power of the priesthood."

The ordained ministry has three levels: deacon, **presbyter** (priest), and bishop. A bishop is the visible head of a number of parishes in a region or diocese. Bishops serve God's family as leaders of the people and priests in their parishes. The bishops are the successors of the apostles. The pope is the successor of Saint Peter, who was the leader of the apostles. Together the bishops and the pope share in the apostolic responsibility and mission of the Church.

Special Duties

Deacons, priests, and bishops each have specific ways they serve communities. What do you know about their duties? On a separate sheet of paper, write the different ways deacons, priests, and bishops serve.

Did You Know?

Charisms are gifts of the Holy Spirit that help members of the Church serve the common good. Among these are the gifts of teaching, proclaiming the gospel, giving to those who are poor, and showing hospitality.

GO TO PAGE 250

Prayer

A Prayer for Guidance

Holiness is our everyday attitude. Whether we serve as priests or laypeople, as teachers or students, we are all called to lives of holiness.

This prayer may help remind you that God will always be with you to guide you along your unique path in life. Pray it silently to yourself.

God, my creator, my provider,
As I struggle to seek the right way in life,
Help my heart find guidance in your love.
Help my mind reflect the depth of your wisdom.
Help my hands create peace.
Help my feet support hope.
And strengthen my love for you,
As I grow strong in your love for me.
Amen.

Pray the prayer again. Which words or phrases stand out? Spend time discussing them with God. Listen to God with your heart.

Sacraments of Service

Read the clues. Write the correct words in the blanks to complete the puzzle.

1. one of the three levels of ordained ministry
   ___ ___ ___ S ___ ___ ___ ___

2. one who celebrates Mass on Sunday
   ___ ___ ___ E ___ ___

3. the sacrament in which men become priests
   ___ ___ ___ ___   ___ R ___ ___ ___ ___

4. a way of life to which God calls people
   V ___ ___ ___ ___ ___ ___ ___

5. a covenant between God and a man and a woman
   ___ ___ ___ ___ ___ I ___ ___ ___ ___

6. another type of ordained minister
   ___ ___ ___ C ___ ___

7. Wedding rings are a symbol of this.
   ___ ___ ___ E ___ ___ ___ ___

Faith Summary

Although every person is called to the vocation of a holy life, some people are called to holiness through Holy Orders or through Matrimony. These sacraments are celebrations of people who have chosen to make a public commitment to service and holiness.

Word I Learned

presbyter

Ways of Being Like Jesus

By listening to God's word, Jesus answered his calling and served others. *Follow your vocation or calling in life—whatever it may be—through holiness and service to others.*

Prayer

Thank you, God, for making it possible for me to live a holy life by serving others with love.

With My Family

Activity Think about something you feel God has called you to do. Write a few sentences to tell how you can live out God's call in your daily life. Have family members share their thoughts. Pray together asking God to help you answer his call.

Faith on the Go Ask one another: *What do you think answering a call to be a priest or a member of a religious order involves?*

Family Prayer *Dear God, bless our family and help all parents to be good models of faith, hope, and charity.*

Think about an outdoor place that has a special meaning for you. Describe that place and explain how it makes you feel.

Caring for the Earth

Prayer

God, my Creator, help me see you in all of creation so that I will praise you and remember to care for the earth.

Our God-Given Responsibility

In the first creation story, God created man and woman. God gave them dominion over the fish of the sea, the birds of the air, and all living things that move on the earth. What exactly does *dominion* mean? It is control or rule. Dominion sounds like an amazing gift, but God gave human beings more than everything on the earth. He gave us something else—responsibility. He entrusted us with the responsibility of caring for his magnificent creation.

Ruling with Love and Wisdom

Pope John Paul II wrote in an **encyclical** that "the dominion granted to man by the Creator is not an absolute power." God wants us to uphold the moral law in our relationships with one another. He also expects us to uphold the moral law in caring for our natural world. God did not intend for us to abuse or misuse natural resources. He wants us to lovingly care for everything in the world around us.

One way to understand the human family's dominion over everything on the earth is to think about how God has dominion over us. God cares for us with love and wisdom. In the same way, our dominion over the planet should show great love and wisdom for nature. We should work to protect all creatures, resources, and habitats. Care for creation is an important principle of Catholic Social Teaching. We show our respect for God when we show care for all that he created.

Environmental Abuse

On a separate sheet of paper, give examples of how people have misused plants, animals, or other natural resources in your local environment.

Solidarity

Our responsibility to care for God's creation requires us to exercise moderation by using only what we need. Think about all the food and water we waste in a single day. Think about people in your own community and all over the world who do not have enough food to eat or water to drink. As Catholics we are called to live in solidarity, or unity, with people in all parts of the world. God calls us to be aware of the needs and rights of people who are less fortunate than we are. We are called to do what we can to help them protect and care for their environments. We are called to provide food, water, and healthy living conditions for those in need.

In the Bible there is no division between justice toward people and justice toward the environment. The Scriptures speak of the natural world as though it is a person—it can rejoice or mourn. The seven themes of Catholic Social Teaching emphasize the concepts of solidarity, dignity, and respect. We are called to love and serve others as part of our faith journey just as Jesus did.

Reading God's Word

Let the heavens be glad and the earth rejoice;
    let the sea and what fills it resound;
    let the plains be joyful and all that is in them.
Then let all the trees of the forest rejoice
    before the Lord who comes,
    who comes to govern the earth,
To govern the world with justice
    and the peoples with faithfulness.

Psalms 96:11–13

GO TO PAGE 251

Prayer

Loving God's Creation

Quietly pray this prayer and then read the reflection that follows.

Act of Love

O my God, I love you above all things with my whole heart and soul, because you are all good and worthy of all my love. I love my neighbor as myself for the love of you. I forgive all who have injured me and I ask pardon of those whom I have injured. Amen.

Now reflect on the love that God has asked us to have for all life. God has given care of the earth to us. Think about the small things you can do to make sure that the gift of creation can continue to be shared by people all over the world. Reflect on how you show your love of God by caring for creation and your neighbors who share it with you.

Exercise Your Dominion!

Imagine that your home is in the center of a circle with a radius of one mile. Now imagine that you are in a helicopter looking out over that area. Sketch a diagram of everything that lies within a mile of your home. Include everything you can think of—animals, plants, buildings, streets, and any natural areas such as forest preserves, fields, or bodies of water.

After you have finished your drawing, think about some of the places in your neighborhood where you could improve the environment. Are there any parks or alleys in your neighborhood that need to be cleaned? Is there an unused piece of land where you could start a community garden? Mark these places on your drawing.

Faith Summary

Pope John Paul II wrote an encyclical that calls us to remember that all of creation is a gift from God and that we have a responsibility to use the gifts of the earth in ways that honor God. By increasing our solidarity with people all over the world, we can work to bring about environmental and social justice.

Word I Learned

encyclical

Ways of Being Like Jesus

Jesus saw the goodness in God's creation. *Respect the natural world and recognize the presence of God in every living thing.*

Prayer

Creator God, thank you for this marvelous world you have made. Show me how to care for it with love and wisdom, now and for the future.

With My Family

Activity Go on a short field trip with your family—to a park, a national forest, a river, or a lake. Find a private area where you can stand together and pray that people will care for the plants and animals that live there.

Faith on the Go Ask one another: *What is one thing we can do in our family to show that we are using our God-given dominion to care for our world?*

Family Prayer *Creator of all things, teach us to be responsible stewards of the people and environments you have given us.*

Community Justice

God created us to live in communities. It is very important for the groups in any community to follow God's **natural law** of justice. For example, governments should support the basic rights of individuals. Laws should direct and encourage people to treat one another fairly, as equals. Our local, state, national, and world leaders should exercise authority with a sense of responsibility and morality.

All people are of equal value in God's eyes. Unfortunately life circumstances are certainly not equal. God calls us to work for those who are poor or in need. These should be the goals of society: to help one another and to promote respect and peace.

Governments can help with this goal by protecting basic rights—the right to religious liberty, the right to personal freedom, the right to access necessary information from the media, the right to life, and the right to be protected from terror and torture.

In the News

Think about world events that you have been hearing about in the news.

What problems are related to the right of people to be treated as equals?

_____

_____

What problems seem to be related to poverty?_____

_____

What problems seem to be related to a loss of freedom?_____

_____

GO TO PAGE 252

A Promise of Mercy

We pray the Magnificat at every evening prayer. In this song and prayer, Mary expressed her own sense of justice after learning that she would give birth to a special child.

The Magnificat

All: *My soul proclaims the greatness of the Lord,*
my spirit rejoices in God my Savior;
for he has looked with favor on his lowly servant.

Group A: *From this day all generations will call me blessed:*
the Almighty has done great things for me,
and holy is his Name.

Group B: *He has mercy on those who fear him*
in every generation.
He has shown the strength of his arm,
he has scattered the proud in their conceit.

Group A: *He has cast down the mighty from their thrones,*
and has lifted up the lowly.

Group B: *He has filled the hungry with good things,*
and the rich he has sent away empty.

All: *He has come to the help of his servant Israel*
for he has remembered his promise of mercy,
the promise he made to our fathers,
to Abraham and his children forever.

Talk to God quietly and thank him for the gifts that he has given Mary and you.

Faith That Works

Catholic Social Teaching highlights ways in which God calls us to live in today's world. God calls us to show justice, respect, dignity, and solidarity in all our communities. As Catholics we share our faith with others through our words and actions.

The Letter of James explores the theme of faith and good deeds by explaining that faith without action is meaningless.

> "What good is it, my brothers, if someone says he has faith but does not have works?" *James 2:14*

He goes on to explain that our faith must lead to good works that help other people. If we do not treat people with dignity and respect, what is the point of having faith at all?

What Do the Scriptures Say?

Read James 2:14–26 and answer these questions.

1. What example does James give of faith that is not followed by good works? _____

_____

_____

2. What does he call faith without works? _____

_____

3. What work justified Abraham? _____

_____

4. What did Abraham need to have before he could ever give up his son?

_____

_____

Faith Summary

God calls us to treat everyone with respect and justice. Our faith leads us to help every person gain fundamental rights such as freedom and religious liberty. By following the example of Jesus, we help the global community by showing compassion for others and by working for justice.

Words I Learned

natural law

Ways of Being Like Jesus

Jesus showed that all people are capable of good and are deserving of our respect. *Treat all people with the same love and respect.*

Prayer

Jesus, thank you for showing me that I have the ability to make my community a place of peace and justice.

With My Family

Activity Visit a local community organization such as a food pantry or a homeless shelter. Find out how your family can help.

Faith on the Go Ask one another: *What would the world be like if everyone lived in peace and had equal rights?*

Family Prayer Loving God, we pray that all people are treated with dignity, respect, and love in our community and around the world.

Celebrating Easter

Easter is the season in the Church's liturgical year when we celebrate Jesus' Resurrection and Ascension. All the sadness of his Death on the cross is washed away as we welcome the risen Christ into our lives. The season of Lent comes to an end with the Mass of the Lord's Supper on the evening of Holy Thursday.

The Easter season begins with the celebration of the Easter Vigil on Holy Saturday and ends on Pentecost Sunday, 50 days later. During the Easter season, we also celebrate the Feast of the Ascension, the day Jesus ascended into heaven.

The word *Easter* has its roots in ancient times. Many believe that it relates to springtime celebrations and the beginning of new life. Today, when we hear the word, we think of Jesus' Resurrection. Every spring we joyfully celebrate Jesus' victory over death and the gift of new life it breathes into us.

Prayer

Dear Jesus, help me to understand the gift of Salvation you have given us. Be with me as I try to care for all your creation.

We Celebrate Our Salvation During Easter

Easter is a time to celebrate the great story of our **Salvation**, God's gift of forgiveness. God's people, our ancestors, awaited the coming of the Savior. As foretold by the prophets, Jesus, the Son of God, came into our world, died on the cross to rescue us from sin, and arose from the dead. As one family in Jesus, all who have come before us and all who will come after us are saved by his Death, Resurrection, and Ascension.

How are we to respond to this amazing gift of Salvation? God created everyone and everything on earth, and it is our duty to care for it. Unfortunately we don't always respect our natural world. We have polluted, endangered the habitats of animals, and put our planet at risk. God wants us to be better keepers of the earth. Let's set an example and do all that we can to protect God's creation.

Our Pledge

We promise to love our earth and everything on it as much as God does from this day forward. We will strive to become better caretakers in our everyday lives. We pledge to recycle, avoid littering, conserve water, use electricity wisely, walk or ride our bikes when we can, and learn more about how our actions affect the planet. We promise to do these things in God's name. Examine the pictures to the right. List what you can do to care for God's creation.

I can _____

_____

I can _____

_____

I can _____

_____

Reading God's Word

Have dominion over the fish of the sea, the birds of the air, and all the living things that move on the earth. *Genesis 1:28*

Mass During Easter

During the Easter season, the Mass celebrates Jesus' Resurrection, his time with his disciples, his Ascension into Heaven, and Pentecost. During the Easter Vigil, we hear the story of our Salvation. The Church celebrates this liturgy on Holy Saturday. The Easter Vigil has four parts. During the Service of Light, we welcome the light of Christ. Next, we hear God's Word from the beginning of time during the Liturgy of the Word. Then we welcome new members into the Church during the Liturgy of Baptism. Finally we receive the Body and Blood of Christ during the Liturgy of the Eucharist.

What We Experience

When you attend church during the Easter season, you will notice white altar linens and vestments. White is the liturgical color of the season. You will see large white Easter lilies, bouquets of spring flowers, and potted plants, all part of God's creation, decorating the sanctuary. You will see the flames flickering on the candles and see holy water to bless yourself. Your church is full of color, beauty, and life to celebrate our Salvation through Jesus.

Did You Know?

The word *Pentecost* means "fiftieth" and comes from the Greek language.

GO TO PAGE 253

Faith Summary

The Easter season begins on Holy Saturday, when we celebrate the Easter Vigil, continues through the Feast of the Ascension, when Jesus ascended to Heaven, and ends on Pentecost, when God sent the Holy Spirit to Jesus' disciples. The Easter Vigil tells the story of our Salvation History beginning with creation, and we respond with a commitment to care for the earth and all its inhabitants.

Word I Learned

Salvation

Ways of Being Like Jesus

Jesus loved and cared for all types of people. *Be kind and respectful to everyone.*

Prayer

Dear God, thank you for the gift of Salvation through your Son, Jesus. Please help us to always care and respect all things in creation.

With My Family

Activity When you go to Mass during Easter, look around your church and find examples of the ideas described on page 149. Talk about what you see.

Faith on the Go Ask one another: *What part of God's creation has the most meaning to you?*

Family Prayer Use Easter to invite family members to grow by praying together for all of God's creation. Ask God to be with your family as you do your best each day to protect the earth.

The Year in Our Church

Liturgical Calendar

The liturgical calendar shows us the feasts and seasons of the Church year.

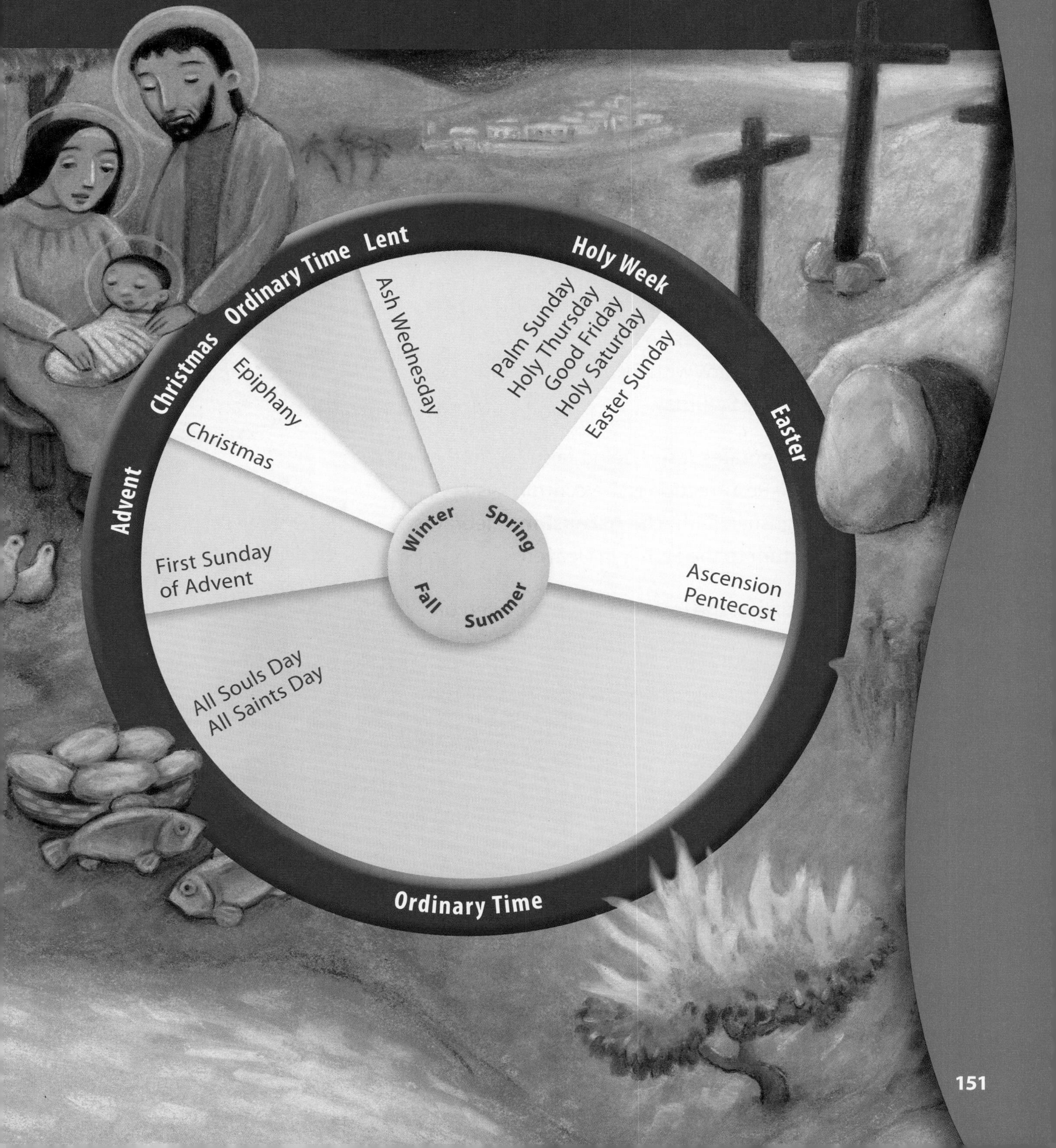
Advent
Christmas
Ordinary Time
Lent
Holy Week
Easter
Ordinary Time
First Sunday of Advent
Christmas
Epiphany
Ash Wednesday
Palm Sunday
Holy Thursday
Good Friday
Holy Saturday
Easter Sunday
Ascension
Pentecost
All Souls Day
All Saints Day
Winter
Spring
Summer
Fall

Liturgical Year

Advent marks the beginning of the Church year. It is a time of anticipation of Christmas and begins four Sundays before the feast.

The Christmas season includes **Christmas,** the celebration of Jesus' birth, and Epiphany, the celebration of his manifestation to the world.

Lent is a season of conversion that begins on Ash Wednesday. It is a time of turning toward God in preparation for Easter.

During **Holy Week** we recall the events leading to the suffering and Death of Jesus. Holy Week begins with Palm Sunday and ends on Holy Saturday.

Easter celebrates Jesus' being raised from the dead. The Resurrection is the central mystery of the Christian faith. The **Ascension** celebrates Jesus' return to the Father in Heaven.

The coming of the Holy Spirit is celebrated on **Pentecost.** With this feast the Easter season ends.

All Saints Day celebrates the victory of all the holy people in Heaven. On **All Souls Day,** we pray for those who have died but are still in Purgatory.

The time set aside for celebrating our call to follow Jesus day by day as his disciples is **Ordinary Time.**

Advent

During Advent we remember how the People of God awaited the birth of the Messiah, and we prepare ourselves to celebrate the birth of Jesus.

Advent lasts four weeks. For many of us, four weeks can seem like a long time to wait. The People of God lived in hope of the coming of the Messiah for hundreds of years.

Prayer

Loving God, help me spend the season of Advent remembering your promise to send a Messiah. Help me to prepare to celebrate the birth of your only Son, Jesus.

John the Baptist

This year we are studying the people and events in the Old Testament. The Old Testament tells the history of the People of God as God prepared them to receive the Messiah. The covenant with Abraham and Sarah, the Exodus, the formation of Israel and the Temple, and the work of the prophets all anticipate the arrival of the Messiah.

John the Baptist was the last prophet to proclaim the arrival of Jesus. He told people that he himself was the messenger promised by the prophet Isaiah. With the help of the Holy Spirit, John prepared people to receive the Messiah.

John Prepares the Way

This is what the Bible says about John the Baptist.

St. John the Baptist, Giovanni Antonio da Pesaro (fl. 1462–1511).

As it is written in Isaiah the prophet:

"Behold, I am sending my messenger ahead of you;
   he will prepare your way.
A voice of one crying out in the desert:
   'Prepare the way of the Lord, make straight his paths.'"

John [the] Baptist appeared in the desert proclaiming a baptism of repentance for the forgiveness of sins. People of the whole Judean countryside and all the inhabitants of Jerusalem were going out to him and were being baptized by him in the Jordan River as they acknowledged their sins. John was clothed in camel's hair, with a leather belt around his waist. He fed on locusts and wild honey. And this is what he proclaimed: "One mightier than I is coming after me. I am not worthy to stoop and loosen the thongs of his sandals. I have baptized you with water; he will baptize you with the holy Spirit."

Mark 1:2–8

Jesse Tree

During Advent many people celebrate Jesus' ancestry by making Jesse trees. A Jesse tree is a bare-branch tree that has ornaments on it representing prophecies, people, and events leading up to the birth of Jesus. The idea for a Jesse tree comes from a verse in Isaiah.

> But a shoot shall sprout from the stump of Jesse,
>   and from his roots a bud shall blossom.   *Isaiah 11:1*

As a group you may want to make a Jesse tree. Your group will need a tree branch that is two or three feet tall. Decorate the tree with illustrated ornaments to represent people such as Noah, Abraham, Isaiah, Mary, John the Baptist, David, and Ruth.

Prayer Service

Leader: Today we remember the people who came before Jesus to prepare his way.

Group A: We remember how God made a covenant with Sarah and Abraham and promised that they would be the founders of a great people.

All: We thank you, God, for fulfilling all that you promised.

Group B: We remember Moses, who was selected by God to lead the Chosen People out of slavery.

Group A: We remember the Old Testament prophets who preached social justice and of the coming of the Messiah.

Group B: We remember John the Baptist, who prepared the people to receive Jesus.

Leader: God, our Father, we remember all the people who waited for the coming of your Son, Jesus. May this Jesse tree remind us of all those who patiently awaited the arrival of the Messiah.

All: Thanks be to God.

Christmas

The season of Christmas is the time when we remember the promises God fulfilled when he gave us his only Son, Jesus. It is also the season to share Jesus' message of love with the world.

Prayer

Gracious God, help me spend the Christmas season remembering the gift that you gave to us when you sent us your only Son, Jesus.

Presentation in the Temple,
Giovanni Bellini, 15th century.

The Presentation at the Temple

Jesus was born into a poor family. The customary way to celebrate the birth of an Israelite couple's son was to present him to God at temple.

When Mary and Joseph entered the Temple, two people, Simeon and Anna, greeted them and rejoiced at the sight of the baby Jesus. They recognized Jesus as the Messiah who would fulfill not only their own hopes but also the hopes of the entire world. This is what Simeon said after he saw Jesus.

> "Now, Master, you may let your servant go in peace,
>   according to your word,
> for my eyes have seen your salvation,
>   which you prepared in sight of all the peoples,
> a light for revelation to the Gentiles,
>   and glory for your people Israel."

The child's father and mother were amazed at what was said about him; and Simeon blessed them and said to Mary his mother, "Behold, this child is destined for the fall and rise of many in Israel, and to be a sign that will be contradicted (and you yourself a sword will pierce) so that the thoughts of many hearts may be revealed."

Luke 2:29–35

Sharing Jesus' Presence

During the Christmas season, we celebrate God's love. We remember the Messiah, the Son of God who became man, God's gift to the world. We also celebrate our mission to bring love to others, especially those most in need of love. We are challenged during Christmas to share the presence of Jesus with all people.

Peace Chain

We celebrate the birth of Jesus on December 25. Seven days after his birth, his parents took him to the Temple. On this day, January 1, people all over the world celebrate World Peace Day, and the pope issues his yearly message for world peace.

In honor of Jesus' message of peace and the pope's message to all of us on World Peace Day, make a Peace Chain with your group. Each of you will make a paper chain link out of green or red construction paper. On your link write a verse from the Bible that is about peace. Several suggested passages are listed below; however, feel free to use a Scripture passage of your own choosing. Decorate your link and then attach it to someone else's finished link. Hang up the entire chain when everyone is finished.

Passages of Peace

▶ Psalm 29:11
▶ Psalm 34:14
▶ Isaiah 52:7
▶ Matthew 5:9
▶ 1 Corinthians 14:33
▶ James 3:18

"The pillars of true peace are justice and that form of love which is forgiveness."

Leader: *As Christmas approaches let us reflect on the meaning of the birth of Jesus by remembering the joy that Simeon and Anna felt when they recognized Jesus as the Son of God.*

Reader: *A reading from the holy Gospel according to Luke.* [Luke 2:29–32]

The Gospel of the Lord.

All: *Praise to you, Lord Jesus Christ.*

Leader: *We share the joy that Anna and Simeon felt when they saw the baby Jesus in the Temple. They had been waiting a long time for the Messiah, but they never gave up hope. They knew that God's promise to send his only Son would be fulfilled.*

All: *God, like Simeon and Anna, we remember your promise to send your only Son, Jesus Christ, to the world. Help us remember to welcome Jesus just as Simeon and Anna did, with gladness in our hearts.*

Leader: *Jesus Christ, you help us to accept God in our lives.*

All: *Thank you for showing us the way.*

Leader: *You help us to love others as God loves us.* ℟.

Leader: *You help us to bring healing to those who are in need.* ℟.

Leader: *You help us to bring peace to the world.* ℟.

Leader: *Let's spend a few minutes telling God how happy we are that he sent his only Son, Jesus Christ.*

Lent

Lent is the time we spend preparing ourselves for Easter. During this 40-day period, we remember the 40 days Jesus spent in the wilderness, fasting and praying. Like Jesus we are called to make sacrifices to help us grow closer to God. What will you do during Lent that brings you closer to God?

Prayer

Loving God, help me spend the season of Lent in prayer and sacrifice so that I may grow closer to you.

Jesus in the Desert

After John baptized Jesus in the Jordan River, the Holy Spirit led Jesus to the harsh desert wilderness, where he ate nothing for 40 days. On the final night, the devil came to test Jesus' faith and trust in God. Just as the Holy Spirit had sustained Jesus through hunger, the Holy Spirit would sustain him through temptation.

First, the devil tempted Jesus with food, knowing that Jesus was hungry. The devil showed Jesus some large stones, saying, "If you are the Son of God, command that these stones become loaves of bread." Jesus refused to be tempted and said, "It is written, 'One does not live by bread alone.'"

Then the devil took Jesus to the top of a high mountain. He showed Jesus all of the kingdoms of the world and told Jesus that he could be king of all those kingdoms if only he would worship the devil. Again, Jesus refused. Jesus said, "It is written: 'You shall worship the Lord, your God, and him alone shall you serve.'"

Finally, the devil took Jesus to the top of a high tower at the Temple in Jerusalem. The devil tried to trick him again by telling Jesus to jump from the tower if he was certain that God's angels could catch him. Jesus refused to do this as well. He said, "It also says, 'You shall not put the Lord, your God, to the test.'"

After that final test, the devil left him, and Jesus returned from the desert.

adapted from Luke 4:1–13

Growing Closer to God

We mark the beginning of Lent by receiving ashes on our foreheads at a special ceremony. During Lent we think about those 40 days and nights Jesus spent in the desert. We see his act of fasting as a sign of his willingness to identify with those who are poor and weak. We hope that, by following his example, we too may identify with people in need so that we may free ourselves from personal wants in order to serve others with charitable acts.

Like Jesus we turn our attention to God during Lent by praying and making small personal sacrifices, such as giving up certain foods. At the age of 14, we are required to give up eating meat on Fridays during Lent. Reading parts of the Bible, praying, and attending Mass as often as we can are also ways that we can celebrate Lent.

Another Lenten practice is giving alms or gifts to those in need. Like prayer and fasting, giving alms focuses our attention on God by emphasizing our dependence on his gifts, which are to be shared with all.

Leader: *Let us praise God. Blessed be God forever.*

All: *Blessed be God forever.*

Leader: *God, as we enter into the season of Lent, help us to resist the temptations of the world, just as your only Son, Jesus, resisted the devil in the desert.*

All: *God, let us spend Lent growing closer to you as we pray, reading your word in the Bible, and resisting temptation, just as your Son, Jesus, resisted the temptations of the devil when he was in the desert.*

Reader: *A reading from the holy Gospel according to Luke.* [Luke 4:1–13]

The Gospel of the Lord.

All: *Praise to you, Lord Jesus Christ.*

Leader: *Let us take time to remember the good things we have done to celebrate Lent. Spend a few minutes telling God the things we have done to observe Lent and ways we will observe Lent in the week to come. Thank you for sending your only Son, Jesus, to help us turn from sin.*

All: *Help us to use prayer and sacrifice to grow closer to you as we observe the season of Lent.*

Holy Week

Holy Week is a time when we remember Jesus' passing from death to new life. It is also a time to reflect on how Jesus, through prayer, was able to make the difficult decision to follow God's will. During this Holy Week, how will you grow closer to God in prayer? What can you do to follow God's will better?

Prayer

Almighty God, give me the strength and courage to listen to you and to obey your will, just as your Son did.

Jesus Prays in the Garden

After the Last Supper, Jesus knew that he had important tasks to finish. He went with Peter, James, and John to pray at a place called Gethsemane, a garden just outside Jerusalem. Jesus told the others to keep watch while he went away and prayed. He asked God whether it was possible for the hour of his death to pass him by. Jesus prayed, "Father, all things are possible to you. Take this cup away from me, yet not what I will but what you will."

When Jesus came back, he found the apostles sleeping. He asked them, "Are you asleep? Could you not keep watch for one hour? Watch and pray that you may not undergo the test. The spirit is willing but the flesh is weak." Jesus then returned to prayer.

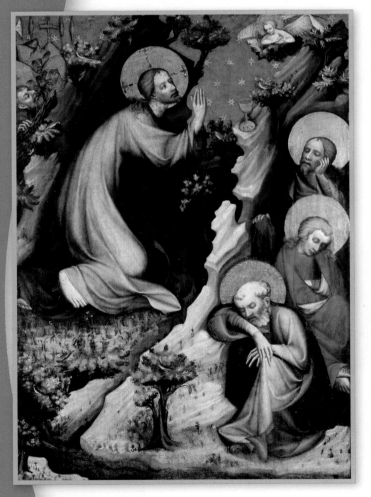

Jesus in the Garden of Gethsemane,
from the Trebon Altarpiece, c. 1380.

Jesus went back to the apostles a second time and found them sleeping again. He returned to his prayers. When he finished praying, he returned a third time and said to them, "Are you still sleeping and taking your rest? It is enough. The hour has come. Behold, the Son of Man is to be handed over to sinners. Get up, let us go. See, my betrayer is at hand."

adapted from Mark 14:32–42

Jesus was ready to follow God's plan. Soon Judas would betray Jesus, Jesus would be brought to trial and crucified, and Jesus would rise from the dead to gain new life for all.

Obeying God's Will

As we see in this Scripture passage, Jesus was totally focused on doing his Father's will. He is troubled and distressed, but he knows that all things are possible with God. In prayer to God, he said, "Not what I will but what you will." When he knew that the hour of his betrayal had come, he woke his disciples, who did not have the strength to watch and pray.

We often find ourselves struggling to make the right decisions in difficult situations. Although we are called to act in obedience to God when making these difficult choices, our obedience is not meant to be simply mechanical. Obedience to God is the result of listening to him and connecting our hearts with his love. We can find the strength needed to make difficult choices by asking Jesus to help.

Prayer Service

Leader: *The grace of our Lord Jesus Christ be with us all, now and forever.*

All: *Amen.*

Leader: *As we prepare for Holy Week and Easter, let us remember the story of Jesus in Gethsemane.*

All: *God, help us find the courage and the strength to follow your will, just as Jesus did when he found the courage and the strength to obey your will and die on the cross for our sins.*

Reader: *A reading from the holy Gospel according to Mark.* [Mark 14:32–42]

The Gospel of the Lord.

All: *Praise to you, Lord Jesus Christ.*

Leader: *Let us take a few minutes to talk to God about a dilemma we face and how we can find the strength and the courage to follow God's will.*

Thank you for helping us turn from sin and follow your will.

All: *Amen.*

Easter and Ascension

After Jesus' Resurrection and Ascension, his followers were prepared to proclaim everything they had witnessed and to spread the Good News from Jerusalem to the entire world.

Prayer

Risen Savior, as we celebrate Easter, help us remember to live out our faith every day while we await your return.

The Disciples Bear Witness

Before Jesus left them, the disciples had questions about the future of Israel. The kingdom of Israel had been destroyed, and the country was controlled by Rome. Prophets had told the people that the Messiah would restore the kingdom, so Jesus' followers wanted to know whether Jesus would restore the kingdom of Israel right away or sometime in the future.

Jesus answered that they should be patient and wait for God to reveal his plan: "It is not for you to know the times or seasons that the Father has established by his own authority. But you will receive the power when the Holy Spirit comes upon you, and you will be my witnesses in Jerusalem, throughout Judea and Samaria, and to the ends of the earth."

Then something truly incredible happened: Jesus rose up into the air, and a cloud took him out of their sight. Jesus' followers were amazed. They stood, staring into the sky where Jesus had disappeared. Then two angels appeared and reminded Jesus' followers that they had work to do: "Men of Galilee, why are you standing there looking at the sky? This Jesus who has been taken up from you into Heaven will return in the same way as you have seen him going into Heaven."

Jesus' followers listened and returned to Jerusalem.

adapted from
Acts of the Apostles 1:6–12

The Ascension, from the *Hours of Etienne Chevalier*, c. 1445, vellum.

Living Out Our Faith

Jesus' words to his followers before he ascended into Heaven convey an important message. These words remind us that we should not spend our time thinking about when Jesus will return. Instead, we should live our faith by helping others and by discovering God's presence in every aspect of life.

Renewing Our Baptismal Promises

When a baby is baptized, his or her parents answer these three questions for the child with "I do."

▶ Do you believe in God, the Father almighty, Creator of Heaven and earth?

▶ Do you believe in Jesus Christ, his only Son, our Lord, who was born of the Virgin Mary, was crucified, died, and was buried, rose from the dead, and is now seated at the right hand of the Father?

▶ Do you believe in the Holy Spirit, the holy Catholic Church, the Communion of Saints, the forgiveness of sins, the resurrection of the body, and the life everlasting?

As we grow we reaffirm these promises at important times and on special days, such as our First Communion, Confirmation, and Easter Sunday. Think about the meaning of these promises and write on a separate sheet of paper a short prayer that expresses how you will serve the world according to these promises. Think about how you can do God's work by helping others.

Leader: *Let us praise our loving God. Blessed be God forever.*

All: *Blessed be God forever.*

Leader: *As we observe Easter, let us remember that God wants us to live our faith in everything we do.*

All: *God, help us to live our faith by reading the Bible, praying, helping others, and following your commandments.*

Reader: *A reading from Acts of the Apostles. [Acts 1:6–12]*

The Word of the Lord.

All: *Thanks be to God.*

Leader: *Let us spend a few minutes reflecting on how we will live out our baptismal promises and be Jesus' witnesses.*

All: *God, encourage us to live our faith this week by helping people who are in need.*

Pentecost

The disciples felt as if they could do anything when the Holy Spirit came to them after Jesus ascended. The Holy Spirit entered their hearts and gave them the strength to carry out the mission Jesus had entrusted to them. We celebrate the gift of the Holy Spirit on the Feast of Pentecost.

Prayer

Father of Light, help me find strength in the Holy Spirit as I live out my faith.

173

God's Spirit Encourages the Exiled Jews

During the Pentecost vigil, we often read from the Old Testament Book of Ezekiel. Although this message was for the exiled Jews in Babylon, it continues to remind us of the presence of the Holy Spirit in our lives.

In 597 B.C. the Babylonians conquered Jerusalem, captured many of the Israelites, and took them to Babylon. The people who were taken lost everything—their homes, the Temple, and their families.

Imagine how discouraged the people felt. During this time God called on Ezekiel to be a prophet who would give hope to the Israelites. The prophet told them that God had shown him a vision of a plain covered with dried bones. In the vision God had asked him, "How can these bones come back to life?"

Ezekiel had responded, "LORD God, you alone know that."

Then God had said, "Prophesy over these bones, and say to them: Dry bones, hear the word of the LORD! . . . I will bring spirit into you, that you may come to life."

When the Israelites heard Ezekiel, they realized that God had not abandoned them. They knew that God would send the spirit to end their discouragement and help them build a life in Babylon. Eventually, the Israelites were able to leave Babylon and return to Jerusalem.

adapted from Ezekiel 37:1–12

In the same way, the Holy Spirit gives us the strength and power to live out our faith, especially when we are discouraged.

The Fruits of the Holy Spirit

The Spirit that gave the exiled Jews strength is the same Spirit that Jesus' followers received at Pentecost. The Holy Spirit gave the apostles the power and encouragement to begin preaching the Good News.

When we are baptized, we receive the Holy Spirit permanently in our lives. With the presence of the Holy Spirit, we are empowered and encouraged to live out our faith. Specifically the presence of the Holy Spirit in our lives helps us to express the Fruits of the Holy Spirit.

In the Letter to the Galatians, 5:22–23, these fruits are named.

- **love:** the charity we express to others
- **joy:** the happiness we receive from our faith
- **peace:** the tranquility of our souls
- **patience:** the ability to endure difficulties
- **kindness:** the goodness we show people
- **generosity:** the ability to share with others
- **faithfulness:** the commitment we make to God
- **gentleness:** the ability to act without harshness or anger
- **self-control:** the ability to avoid acting on temptation

Which of the Fruits of the Holy Spirit do you most need right now? Do you need to be generous to others? Do you need to be more patient with someone?

Leader: *Let us praise the God of wisdom and grace. Blessed be God forever.*

All: *Blessed be God forever.*

Leader: *As we observe Pentecost, let us think about the importance of the Holy Spirit in our lives.*

All: *May the Holy Spirit strengthen and guide us as we live out our faith.*

Reader 1: *A reading from the Book of Ezekiel. [Ezekiel 37:1–6]*

The Word of the Lord.

All: *Thanks be to God.*

Leader: *Let us spend a moment asking the Holy Spirit to dwell in our hearts and to grant us the spiritual gifts that we cherish.*

Reader 2: *Spirit of love, joy, and peace.*

All: *Enter our hearts.*

Reader 3: *Spirit of patience, kindness, and generosity.*

Reader 4: *Spirit of faithfulness, gentleness, and self-control.*

Leader: *God, grant us these Fruits of the Holy Spirit so that others may recognize your presence.*

All Saints Day and All Souls Day

All Saints Day and All Souls Days are celebrated on November 1 and 2. On these days we remember those who have died and who are either in Heaven or in Purgatory.

Prayer

God our Father, thank you for the sacraments, which keep us in contact with you and with all other believers, living and dead.

Celebrating the Saints

The Catholic Church has recognized thousands of individuals as saints for their exceptional commitment to faith and charity.

We look to the saints as role models and leaders; we also ask for their help and guidance in our prayers.

Although the Church has named only specific people as saints, in a larger sense, all of us who believe in Jesus and live virtuous lives are saints. Together we are united with God in the Communion of Saints. The Eucharist especially brings all Christians into a special relationship with God and with one another.

When we are united with Christ, we are able to live virtuous lives, just as the saints did. As a result Christians are set apart in three ways: First, Christians are to know that their first priority must be for things of God. Second, Christians are to live lives of holiness and good works. Third, Christians are to be confident that one day they will live with God forever.

Think of a saint whom you admire. Why do you admire that person so much? What did he or she do for God and for others? Did he or she start a religious order? How was that saint's life virtuous?

Saint Francis of Assisi

Saint Thérèse of Lisieux

Saint Martin de Porres

The Communion of Saints

We celebrate the union of believers on All Saints Day. On this day we remember all those who have gone before us and are now living in God's presence. On All Souls Day, we remember those who have died but whose souls are being prepared in Purgatory to live with God forever. They are on the final part of the journey. We remember these people because we are united to all believers through the sacraments.

Saint Cards

Use the example below to make a card for your favorite saint. On the front of the card, draw a picture of the saint and write a prayer. Then on the back of the card add something about the accomplishments of that saint.

Remember that we are all in communion with the saints, so make a second card for yourself. Draw your picture on the front of the card. On the back put your name, date of birth, and place of birth. Then write some of the good things you have done to show how you are also becoming a saint. Have you helped others? Have you done any service for your community? Do you pray regularly? Write all of those things and any others you can think of.

Margaret was born in 1046 in Hunga
In 1066, as some of the few remainin
Saxon Royals in England, and fearing
for their lives, Margaret's family fled
northwards and landed in Fife. The
Scottish King, Malcolm III, and Margaret
m   1069. Queen Margaret was
            her good influence on her
        so for her devout piety and
            nce. Margaret founded
        teries and pilgrimage
        d Margaret had eight
        aret was known for
        r and orphans.
            vas cannonized in
            ocent IV.

        is celebrated
        of her death,

Margaret of Scotland

Loving God, Thank you for St. Margaret of Scotland. She was a mother, a leader, a teacher, and a servant to those who are poor and helpless. Let her example and prayers help us to do good. Amen.

Leader: *Praise be to God, who fills our lives with joy.*

All: *Praise be to God.*

Leader: *As we observe All Saints Day and All Souls Day, let us remember that God unites all his followers, living and dead, in the Communion of Saints.*

Reader 1: *A reading from the First Letter of John. [1 John 3:1–3]*

The Word of the Lord.

All: *Thanks be to God.*

Leader: *Let us spend a few minutes talking to God. On All Saints Day, we remember those who are living with God. On All Souls Day, we pray for those who are in Purgatory.*

Reader 2: *God, help us to live our faith in service to others so that we may grow closer to you.*

Reader 3: *God, help us follow in the footsteps of the saints, who have shown us how to serve the Kingdom of God right here on earth.*

Reader 4: *God, help us remember those who are already with you in Heaven and help us to pray for those who are still waiting to be with you.*

All: *God, thank you for the sacraments, especially the Sacrament of the Eucharist, which unites us, your followers, in the Communion of Saints.*

Prayers and Practices of Our Faith

Knowing and Praying Our Faith

The Bible and You

God speaks to us in many ways. One way God speaks to us is through the Bible. The Bible is the most important book in Christian life because it is God's message, or Revelation. The Bible is the story of God's promise to care for us, especially through his Son, Jesus. At Mass we hear stories from the Bible. We can also read the Bible on our own.

The Bible is not just one book; it is a collection of many books. The writings in the Bible were inspired by the Holy Spirit and written by many different authors using different styles.

The Bible is made up of two parts: The Old Testament and the New Testament. The Old Testament contains 46 books that tell stories about the Jewish people and their faith in God before Jesus was born.

The first five books of the Old Testament—Genesis, Exodus, Leviticus, Numbers, and Deuteronomy—are referred to as the Torah, meaning "instruction" or "law." The central story in the Torah is the Exodus, the liberation of the Hebrew slaves as Moses led them out of Egypt and to the Promised Land. During the journey God gave the Ten Commandments to Moses and the people. A beautiful part of the Old Testament is the Book of Psalms. A psalm is a prayer in the form of a poem. Each psalm expresses an aspect, or feature, of the depth of human emotion. Over several centuries, 150 psalms were gathered to form the Book of Psalms. They were once sung at the Temple in Jerusalem, and they have been used in the public worship of the Church since its beginning. Catholics also pray the psalms as part of their private prayer and reflection.

The prophets were called by God to speak for him and urge the Jewish people to be faithful to the Covenant. A large part—18 books—of the Old Testament presents the messages and actions of the prophets.

The New Testament contains 27 books that tell the story of Jesus' life, Death, and Resurrection and the experience of the early Christians. For Christians the most important books of the New Testament are the four Gospels—Matthew, Mark, Luke, and John. Many of the 27 books are letters written by leaders such as Saint Paul.

How can you find a passage in the Bible? Bible passages are identified by book, chapter, and verse, for example, Matthew 3:14. The name of the book comes first. Sometimes this is in abbreviated form. Your Bible's table of contents will help you determine what the abbreviation means. For example, Mt stands for Matthew. After the name of the book, there are two numbers. The first number identifies the chapter, which in the example below is chapter 3; it is followed by a colon. The second number identifies the verse or verses, which in the example is verse 14.

Saint Paul has written many books of the Bible.

Locating a Scripture Passage

Chapter 3

Verse 14

Book of Matthew

MATTHEW 3:14

1142

lee to Jor'dan unto John, to be baptized of him. *Matt. 2:22; Luke 3:21*
14 But John forbad him, saying, I have need to be baptized of thee, and comest thou to me?
15 And Je'sus answering said unto him, Suffer *it to be so* now: for thus it becometh us to fulfil all righteousness. Then he suffered him.
★ 16 And Je'sus, when he was baptized, went up straightway out of the water: and, lo, the heavens were opened unto him, and he saw the Spir'it of God descending like a dove, and lighting upon him: *Isa. 11:2*
17 And lo, a voice from heaven,

7 Je'sus again, Th
LORD THY
8 Again into an ex
sheweth h
world, and
9 And
things will
down and
10 Then
thee hence,
THOU SHALT
GOD, AND H
SERVE.
11 Then the o

Prayer and Forms of Prayer

God is always with us. He wants us to talk to him and to listen to him. In prayer we raise our hearts and minds to God. We are able to speak to and listen to God because, through the Holy Spirit, God teaches us how to pray.

We Pray in Many Ways

Because prayer is so important, the Church teaches us to pray often and in many ways. Sometimes we show love or admiration for God (prayer of blessing and adoration). Other times we ask God for something for ourselves (prayer of petition). Sometimes we pray for others (prayer of intercession). We also thank God in prayer (prayer of thanksgiving). Finally we can also praise God (prayer of praise). We can pray silently or aloud. We can pray alone or with others. Praying with others is called communal prayer.

We Meditate and Contemplate

One way to pray is to meditate. To meditate is to think about God. We try to keep our attention and focus on God. In meditation we may use Scripture, prayer books, or icons, which are religious images, to help us concentrate and to spark our imagination.

Another way to pray is to contemplate. This means that we rest quietly in God's presence.

We Get Ready to Pray

We live in a very busy, noisy, and fast-paced world. Sometimes, because of this, we have difficulty concentrating. In order to meditate or reflect, we need to prepare ourselves.

We can get ready for meditation by resting our bodies in a comfortable position. Sitting with our backs straight and both feet on the floor is one comfortable position. We can close our eyes, fold our hands comfortably in front of us, and silently take a deep breath and then let it out slowly. We can establish a rhythm by slowly counting to three while breathing in and slowly counting to three while breathing out. Concentrating on our breathing helps us to quiet our thoughts.

We Avoid Distractions

If we become distracted by thinking about something, such as the day at school or a sports event, we can just go back to thinking about our breathing. After a little practice, we will be able to avoid distractions, pray with our imagination, and spend time with God or Jesus in our hearts.

Prayers to Take to Heart

We can pray with any words that come to mind. Sometimes, when we find that choosing our own words is difficult, we can use traditional prayers. Likewise, when we pray aloud with others, we rely on traditional prayers to unite our minds, hearts, and voices. Memorizing traditional prayers such as the following can be very helpful. When we memorize prayers, we take them to heart, meaning that we not only learn the words but we also try to understand and live them.

Lord's Prayer

Our Father, who art in heaven,
hallowed be thy name;
thy kingdom come,
thy will be done
on earth as it is in heaven.
Give us this day our daily bread,
and forgive us our trespasses,
as we forgive those who trespass against us;
and lead us not into temptation,
but deliver us from evil.

Hail Mary

Hail Mary, full of grace,
the Lord is with you.
Blessed are you among women,
and blessed is the fruit of your womb, Jesus.
Holy Mary, Mother of God,
pray for us sinners,
now and at the hour of our death.
Amen.

Morning Offering

*My God, I offer you my prayers, works, joys,
and sufferings of this day in union with the holy
sacrifice of the Mass throughout the world.
I offer them for all the intentions of your Son's
Sacred Heart, for the salvation of souls,
reparation for sin, and the reunion of Christians.
Amen.*

Prayer Before Meals

*Bless us, O Lord, and these your gifts
which we are about to receive from
   your goodness.
Through Christ our Lord.
Amen.*

Prayer After Meals

*We give you thanks
for all your gifts,
almighty God,
living and reigning
now and for ever.
Amen.*

Act of Contrition

*My God,
I am sorry for my sins with all my heart.
In choosing to do wrong
and failing to do good,
I have sinned against you
whom I should love above all things.
I firmly intend, with your help,
to do penance,
to sin no more,
and to avoid whatever leads me to sin.
Our Savior Jesus Christ
suffered and died for us.
In his name, my God, have mercy.*

Apostles' Creed

I believe in God,

the Father almighty,

Creator of heaven and earth,

and in Jesus Christ, his only Son, our Lord,

who was conceived by the Holy Spirit,

born of the Virgin Mary,

suffered under Pontius Pilate,

was crucified, died and was buried;

he descended into hell;

on the third day he rose again from the dead;

he ascended into heaven,

and is seated at the right hand of God the Father almighty;

from there he will come to judge the living and the dead.

I believe in the Holy Spirit,

the holy catholic Church,

the communion of saints,

the forgiveness of sins,

the resurrection of the body,

and life everlasting. Amen.

Nicene Creed

I believe in one God,
the Father almighty,
maker of heaven and earth,
of all things visible and invisible.

I believe in one Lord Jesus Christ,
the Only Begotten Son of God,
born of the Father before all ages.
God from God, Light from Light,
true God from true God,
begotten, not made, consubstantial with the Father;
through him all things were made.
For us men and for our salvation
he came down from heaven,
and by the Holy Spirit was incarnate of the Virgin Mary,
and became man.

For our sake he was crucified under Pontius Pilate,
he suffered death and was buried,
and rose again on the third day
in accordance with the Scriptures.
He ascended into heaven
and is seated at the right hand of the Father.
He will come again in glory
to judge the living and the dead
and his kingdom will have no end.

I believe in the Holy Spirit, the Lord, the giver of life,
who proceeds from the Father and the Son,
who with the Father and the Son is adored and glorified,
who has spoken through the prophets.

I believe in one, holy, catholic and apostolic Church.
I confess one Baptism for the forgiveness of sins
and I look forward to the resurrection of the dead
and the life of the world to come. Amen.

Act of Faith

O my God, I firmly believe that you are one God in three divine Persons, Father, Son, and Holy Spirit. I believe that your divine Son became man and died for our sins, and that he will come to judge the living and the dead. I believe these and all the truths which the holy Catholic Church teaches, because you have revealed them, who can neither deceive nor be deceived. Amen.

Act of Hope

O my God, relying on your infinite mercy and promises, I hope to obtain pardon of my sins, the help of your grace, and life everlasting, through the merits of Jesus Christ, my Lord and Redeemer. Amen.

Act of Love

O my God, I love you above all things with my whole heart and soul, because you are all good and worthy of all my love. I love my neighbor as myself for the love of you. I forgive all who have injured me and I ask pardon of those whom I have injured. Amen.

Hail, Holy Queen (*Salve Regina*)

Hail, holy Queen, Mother of mercy,
hail, our life, our sweetness, and our hope.
To you we cry, the children of Eve;
to you we send up our sighs,
mourning and weeping in this land of exile.
Turn, then, most gracious advocate,
your eyes of mercy toward us;
lead us home at last
and show us the blessed fruit of your womb, Jesus:
O clement, O loving, O sweet Virgin Mary.

Prayer to the Holy Spirit

Come, Holy Spirit, fill the hearts of your faithful.
And kindle in them the fire of your love.
Send forth your Spirit and they shall be created.
And you will renew the face of the earth.
Let us pray.

Lord,
by the light of the Holy Spirit
you have taught the hearts of your faithful.
In the same Spirit
help us to relish what is right
and always rejoice in your consolation.
We ask this through Christ our Lord.
Amen.

Prayer for Vocations

God, in Baptism you called me by name
and made me a member of your people,
    the Church.
Help all your people to know their vocation
    in life,
and to respond by living a life of holiness.
For your greater glory and for the service
    of your people,
raise up dedicated and generous leaders
who will serve as sisters, priests,
brothers, deacons, and lay ministers.

Send your Spirit to guide and strengthen me
that I may serve your people
following the example of your Son, Jesus Christ,
in whose name I offer this prayer.
Amen.

The Rosary

The Rosary helps us to pray to Jesus through Mary. When we pray the Rosary, we think about the special events, or mysteries, in the lives of Jesus and Mary. The rosary is made up of a string of beads and a crucifix. We hold the crucifix in our hands as we pray the Sign of the Cross. Then we pray the Apostles' Creed. Next to the crucifix, there is a single bead, followed by a set of three beads and another single bead. We pray the Lord's Prayer as we hold the first single bead and a Hail Mary at each bead in the set of three that follows. Then we pray the Glory Be to the Father. On the next single bead, we think about the first mystery and pray the Lord's Prayer.

Madonna of the Rosary, Jacopo Zucchi, c. 1569, oil on canvas.

There are five sets of ten beads; each set is called a decade. We pray a Hail Mary on each bead of a decade as we reflect on a particular mystery in the lives of Jesus and Mary. The Glory Be to the Father is prayed at the end of each set. Between sets is a single bead on which we think about one of the mysteries and pray the Lord's Prayer. In some places people pray the Hail, Holy Queen after the last decade.

We end by holding the crucifix as we pray the Sign of the Cross.

Praying the Rosary

9. Pray ten Hail Marys and one Glory Be to the Father.

10. Think about the fourth mystery. Pray the Lord's Prayer.

8. Think about the third mystery. Pray the Lord's Prayer.

11. Pray ten Hail Marys and one Glory Be to the Father.

7. Pray ten Hail Marys and one Glory Be to the Father.

6. Think about the second mystery. Pray the Lord's Prayer.

12. Think about the fifth mystery. Pray the Lord's Prayer.

5. Pray ten Hail Marys and one Glory Be to the Father.

13. Pray ten Hail Marys and one Glory Be to the Father.

4. Think about the first mystery. Pray the Lord's Prayer.

Pray the Hail, Holy Queen.
Many people pray the Hail, Holy Queen after the last decade.

3. Pray three Hail Marys and one Glory Be to the Father.

2. Pray the Lord's Prayer.

14. Pray the Sign of the Cross.

1. Pray the Sign of the Cross and the Apostles' Creed.

Mysteries of the Rosary

The Church has used three sets of mysteries for many centuries. In 2002 Blessed Pope John Paul II proposed a fourth set of mysteries—the Mysteries of Light, or Luminous Mysteries. According to his suggestion, the four sets of mysteries might be prayed on the following days: the Joyful Mysteries on Monday and Saturday, the Sorrowful Mysteries on Tuesday and Friday, the Glorious Mysteries on Wednesday and Sunday, and the Luminous Mysteries on Thursday.

The Joyful Mysteries

The Joyful Mysteries

1. **The Annunciation** Mary learns that she has been chosen to be the mother of Jesus.
2. **The Visitation** Mary visits Elizabeth, who tells her that she will always be remembered.
3. **The Nativity** Jesus is born in a stable in Bethlehem.
4. **The Presentation** Mary and Joseph take the infant Jesus to the Temple to present him to God.
5. **The Finding of Jesus in the Temple** Jesus is found in the Temple, discussing his faith with the teachers.

The Mysteries of Light

The Mysteries of Light

1. **The Baptism of Jesus in the River Jordan** God proclaims that Jesus is his beloved Son.
2. **The Wedding Feast at Cana** At Mary's request Jesus performs his first miracle.
3. **The Proclamation of the Kingdom of God** Jesus calls all to conversion and service to the kingdom.
4. **The Transfiguration of Jesus** Jesus is revealed in glory to Peter, James, and John.
5. **The Institution of the Eucharist** Jesus offers his Body and Blood at the Last Supper.

The Sorrowful Mysteries

The Sorrowful Mysteries

1. **The Agony in the Garden** Jesus prays in the Garden of Gethsemane on the night before he dies.

2. **The Scourging at the Pillar** Jesus is lashed with whips.

3. **The Crowning with Thorns** Jesus is mocked and crowned with thorns.

4. **The Carrying of the Cross** Jesus carries the cross that will be used to crucify him.

5. **The Crucifixion** Jesus is nailed to the cross and dies.

The Glorious Mysteries

The Glorious Mysteries

1. **The Resurrection** God the Father raises Jesus from the dead.

2. **The Ascension** Jesus returns to his Father in Heaven.

3. **The Coming of the Holy Spirit** The Holy Spirit comes to bring new life to the disciples.

4. **The Assumption of Mary** At the end of her life on earth, Mary is taken body and soul into Heaven.

5. **The Coronation of Mary** Mary is crowned as Queen of Heaven and Earth.

Stations of the Cross

The 14 Stations of the Cross represent events from Jesus' Passion and Death. At each station we use our senses and our imagination to reflect prayerfully on Jesus' suffering, Death, and Resurrection.

1

Jesus Is Condemned to Death.
Pontius Pilate condemns Jesus to death.

2

Jesus Takes Up the Cross.
Jesus willingly accepts and patiently bears the cross.

3

Jesus Falls the First Time.
Weakened by torments and loss of blood, Jesus falls beneath the cross.

4

Jesus Meets His Sorrowful Mother.
Jesus meets his mother, Mary, who is filled with grief.

5

Simon of Cyrene Helps Jesus Carry the Cross.
Soldiers force Simon of Cyrene to carry the cross.

6

Veronica Wipes the Face of Jesus.
Veronica steps through the crowd to wipe the face of Jesus.

7 Jesus Falls the
Second Time.
Jesus falls beneath the
weight of the cross a
second time.

8 Jesus Meets the
Women of Jerusalem.
Jesus tells the women
not to weep for him but
for themselves and for
their children.

9 Jesus Falls
the Third Time.
Weakened almost to
the point of death,
Jesus falls a third time.

10 Jesus Is Stripped of
His Garments.
The soldiers strip
Jesus of his garments,
treating him as a
common criminal.

11 Jesus Is Nailed to
the Cross.
Jesus' hands and
feet are nailed to
the cross.

12 Jesus Dies on
the Cross.
After suffering
greatly on the cross,
Jesus bows his head
and dies.

13 Jesus Is Taken Down
from the Cross.
The lifeless body of Jesus
is tenderly placed in the
arms of Mary, his mother.

14 Jesus Is Laid in
the Tomb.
Jesus' disciples place
his body in the tomb.

The closing
prayer—
sometimes
included as a
15th station—
reflects on the
Resurrection
of Jesus.

Celebrating Our Faith

The Seven Sacraments

Jesus touches our lives through the sacraments. Our celebrations of the sacraments are signs of Jesus' presence in our lives and a means for receiving his grace. The Church celebrates seven sacraments, which are divided into three categories.

Sacraments of Initiation

These sacraments lay the foundation for our lives as Catholics.

Baptism

In Baptism we receive new life in Christ. Baptism takes away Original Sin and gives us a new birth in the Holy Spirit. Its sign is the pouring of water.

Confirmation

Confirmation seals our life of faith in Jesus. Its signs are the laying on of hands on a person's head, most often by a bishop, and the anointing with oil. Like Baptism, Confirmation is received only once.

Eucharist

The Eucharist nourishes our life of faith. Its signs are the Bread and Wine we receive—the Body and Blood of Christ.

Sacraments of Healing

These sacraments celebrate the healing power of Jesus.

Penance and Reconciliation

Through Penance we receive God's forgiveness. Forgiveness requires being sorry for our sins. In Penance we receive Jesus' healing grace through absolution by the priest. The signs of this sacrament are our confession of sins and the words of absolution.

Anointing of the Sick

This sacrament unites a sick person's suffering with that of Jesus and brings forgiveness of sins. Oil, a symbol of strength, is the sign of this sacrament. A person is anointed with oil and receives the laying on of hands from a priest.

Sacraments at the Service of Communion

These sacraments help members serve the community.

Holy Orders

In Holy Orders men are ordained as priests, deacons, or bishops. Priests serve as spiritual leaders of their communities, and deacons serve to remind us of our baptismal call to help others. Bishops carry on the teachings of the apostles. The signs of this sacrament are the laying on of hands and the anointing with oil by the bishop.

Matrimony

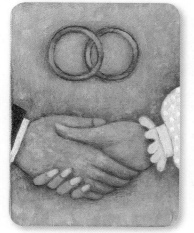

In Matrimony a baptized man and woman are united with each other as a sign of the unity between Jesus and his Church. Matrimony requires the consent of the couple, as expressed in the marriage promises. The couple and their wedding rings are the signs of this sacrament.

Celebrating the Lord's Day

Sunday is the day on which we celebrate the Resurrection of Jesus. Sunday is the Lord's Day. We gather for Mass, rest from work, and perform works of mercy. People all over the world gather at God's eucharistic table as brothers and sisters.

The Order of Mass

The Mass is the high point of the Catholic life, and it always follows a set order.

Introductory Rites—preparing to celebrate the Eucharist

Entrance Chant

We gather as a community and praise God in song.

Greeting

We pray the Sign of the Cross. The priest welcomes us.

Penitential Act

We remember our sins and ask God for mercy.

Gloria

We praise God in song.

Collect

We ask God to hear our prayers.

Liturgy of the Word—hearing God's plan of Salvation

First Reading

We listen to God's Word, usually from the Old Testament.

Responsorial Psalm

We respond to God's Word in song.

Second Reading

We listen to God's Word from the New Testament.

Gospel Acclamation

We sing "Alleluia!" to praise God for the Good News. During Lent we use a different acclamation.

Gospel Reading

We stand and listen to the Gospel of the Lord.

Homily

The priest or the deacon explains God's Word.

Profession of Faith

We proclaim our faith through the Nicene Creed.

Prayer of the Faithful

We pray for our needs and the needs of others.

The Liturgy of the Eucharist—
celebrating Christ's
presence in the Eucharist

Presentation and Preparation of the Gifts

We bring gifts of bread and wine to the altar.

Prayer over the Offerings

The priest prays that God will accept our sacrifice.

Eucharistic Prayer

This prayer of thanksgiving is the center and high point of the entire celebration.

- ▶ **Preface**—We give thanks and praise to God.
- ▶ **Holy, Holy, Holy**—We sing an acclamation of praise.
- ▶ **Institution Narrative**—The Bread and Wine become the Body and Blood of Jesus Christ.
- ▶ **The Mystery of Faith**—We proclaim the mystery of our faith.
- ▶ **Amen**—We affirm the words and actions of the Eucharistic Prayer.

Communion Rite —preparing to receive the Body and Blood of Jesus Christ

The Lord's Prayer

We pray the Lord's Prayer.

Sign of Peace

We offer one another Christ's peace.

Lamb of God

We pray for forgiveness, mercy, and peace.

Communion

We receive the Body and Blood of Jesus Christ.

Prayer after Communion

We pray that the Eucharist will strengthen us to live as Jesus did.

Concluding Rites—going forth to glorify the Lord by our life

Final Blessing

We receive God's blessing.

Dismissal

We go in peace, glorifying the Lord by our lives.

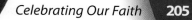

Holy Days of Obligation

The Holy Days of Obligation are the days other than Sundays on which we celebrate the great things God has done for us through Jesus and the saints. On Holy Days of Obligation, Catholics attend Mass.

Six Holy Days of Obligation are celebrated in the United States.

January 1

Mary, Mother of God

40 days after Easter

Ascension

August 15

Assumption of the
Blessed Virgin Mary

November 1

All Saints Day

December 8

Immaculate Conception

December 25

Nativity of
Our Lord Jesus Christ

Precepts of the Church

The Precepts of the Church describe the minimum effort we must make in prayer and in living a moral life. All Catholics are called to move beyond the minimum by growing in love of God and love of neighbor. The Precepts are as follows:

1. attendance at Mass on Sundays and Holy Days of Obligation

2. confession of sin at least once a year

3. reception of Holy Communion at least once a year during the Easter season

4. observance of the days of fast and abstinence

5. providing for the needs of the Church

An Examination of Conscience

An examination of conscience is the act of looking prayerfully into our hearts to ask how we have hurt our relationships with God and with other people through our thoughts, words, and actions. We reflect on the Ten Commandments and the teachings of the Church. The questions below help us in our examination of conscience.

My Relationship with God

What steps am I taking to help me grow closer to God and to others? Do I turn to God often during the day, especially when I am tempted?

Do I participate at Mass with attention and devotion on Sundays and Holy Days of Obligation?

Do I pray often and read the Bible? Do I use God's name and the names of Jesus, Mary, and the saints with love and reverence?

My Relationships with Family, Friends, and Neighbors

Have I set a bad example through my words or actions? Do I treat others fairly? Do I spread stories that hurt other people?

Am I loving of those in my family? Am I respectful of my neighbors, my friends, and those in authority?

Do I show respect for my body and for the bodies of others? Do I keep away from forms of entertainment that do not respect God's gift of sexuality?

Have I taken or damaged anything that did not belong to me? Have I cheated, copied homework, or lied?

Do I quarrel with others just so I can get my own way? Do I insult others to try to make them think they are less than I am? Do I hold grudges and try to hurt people who I think have hurt me?

How to Make a Good Confession

An examination of conscience is an important part of preparing for the Sacrament of Penance and Reconciliation. The Sacrament of Reconciliation includes the following steps:

1. The priest greets us, and we pray the Sign of the Cross. He invites us to trust in God. He may read God's Word with us.

2. We confess our sins. The priest may help and counsel us.

3. The priest gives us a penance to perform. Penance is an act of kindness or prayers to pray, or both.

4. The priest asks us to express our sorrow, usually by reciting the Act of Contrition.

5. We receive absolution. The priest says, "I absolve you from your sins in the name of the Father, and of the Son, and of the Holy Spirit." We respond, "Amen."

6. The priest dismisses us by saying, "Go in peace." We go forth to perform the act of penance he has given us.

Living Our Faith

The Ten Commandments

As believers in Jesus Christ, we are called to a new life and are asked to make moral choices that keep us united with God. With the help and grace of the Holy Spirit, we can choose ways to act to keep us close to God, to help other people, and to be witnesses to Jesus.

The Ten Commandments guide us in making choices that help us to live as God wants us to live. The first three commandments tell us how to love God; the other seven tell us how to love our neighbor.

1. I am the Lord your God: you shall not have strange gods before me.
2. You shall not take the name of the Lord your God in vain.
3. Remember to keep holy the Lord's Day.
4. Honor your father and your mother.
5. You shall not kill.
6. You shall not commit adultery.
7. You shall not steal.
8. You shall not bear false witness against your neighbor.
9. You shall not covet your neighbor's wife.
10. You shall not covet your neighbor's goods.

The Great Commandment

The Ten Commandments are fulfilled in Jesus' Great Commandment:

"You shall love God with all your heart, with all your soul, with all your mind, and with all your strength. You shall love your neighbor as yourself."

adapted from Mark 12:30–31

The New Commandment

Before his Death on the cross, Jesus gave his disciples a
new commandment:

"[L]ove one another. As I have loved you, so you also should love
one another."

John 13:34

The Beatitudes

The Beatitudes are the teachings of Jesus in the Sermon on the Mount
(Matthew 5:3–10). Jesus teaches us that if we live according to the
Beatitudes, we will live a happy Christian life. The Beatitudes fulfill
God's promises made to Abraham and his descendants and describe the
rewards that will be ours as loyal followers of Christ.

Blessed are the poor in spirit,
   for theirs is the kingdom of heaven.

Blessed are they who mourn,
   for they will be comforted.

Blessed are the meek,
   for they will inherit the land.

Blessed are they who hunger and thirst for righteousness,
   for they will be satisfied.

Blessed are the merciful,
   for they will be shown mercy.

Blessed are the clean of heart,
   for they will see God.

Blessed are the peacemakers,
   for they will be called children of God.

Blessed are they who are persecuted
   for the sake of righteousness,
   for theirs is the kingdom of heaven.

Making Good Choices

Our conscience is the inner voice that helps us to know the law God has placed in our hearts. Our conscience helps us to judge the moral qualities of our own actions. It guides us to do good and to avoid evil.

The Holy Spirit can help us form a good conscience. We form our conscience by studying the teachings of the Church and by following the guidance of our parents and pastoral leaders.

God has given every human being freedom of choice. This does not mean that we have the right to do whatever we please. We can live in true freedom if we cooperate with the Holy Spirit, who gives us the virtue of prudence. This virtue helps us recognize what is good in every situation and make correct choices. The Holy Spirit gives us the gifts of wisdom and understanding to help us make the right choices in life in relationship to God and others. The gift of counsel helps us reflect on making correct choices in life.

The Ten Commandments help us to make moral choices that are pleasing to God. We have the grace of the sacraments, the teachings of the Church, and the good example of saints and fellow Christians to help us make good choices.

Making moral choices involves the following steps:

1. Ask the Holy Spirit for help.

2. Think about God's law and the teachings of the Church.

3. Think about what will happen as a result of your choice. Ask yourself, will the consequences be pleasing to God? Will my choice hurt someone else?

4. Seek advice from someone you respect and remember that Jesus is with you.

5. Ask yourself how your choice will affect your relationships with God and with others.

Making moral choices takes into consideration the object of the choice, our intention in making the choice, and the circumstances in which the choice is made. It is never right to make an evil choice in the hope of gaining something good.

Virtues

Virtues are gifts from God that lead us to live in a close relationship with him. Virtues are like habits. They need to be practiced; they can be lost if they are neglected. The three most important virtues are called Theological Virtues, because they come from God and lead to God. The Cardinal Virtues are human virtues, acquired by education and good actions. *Cardinal* comes from *cardo*, the Latin word for *hinge*, meaning "that on which other things depend."

Theological Virtues

faith   hope   charity

Cardinal Virtues

prudence   justice   fortitude   temperance

Gifts of the Holy Spirit

The Holy Spirit makes it possible for us to do what God asks of us by giving us these gifts.

wisdom   understanding   counsel   fortitude
knowledge   piety   fear of the Lord

Fruits of the Holy Spirit

The Fruits of the Holy Spirit are signs of the Holy Spirit's action in our lives.

love

peace

kindness

faithfulness

self-control

joy

patience

generosity

gentleness

Church Tradition also includes goodness, modesty, and chastity as Fruits of the Holy Spirit.

Works of Mercy

The Corporal and Spiritual Works of Mercy are actions we can perform that extend God's compassion and mercy to those in need.

Corporal Works of Mercy

The Corporal Works of Mercy are kind acts by which we help our neighbors with their material and physical needs.

feed the hungry

clothe the naked

bury the dead

shelter the homeless

visit the sick and imprisoned

give alms to the poor

Spiritual Works of Mercy

The Spiritual Works of Mercy are acts of compassion, as listed below, by which we help our neighbors with their emotional and spiritual needs.

instruct

console

forgive

advise

comfort

bear wrongs patiently

Showing Our Love for the World

In the story of the Good Samaritan (Luke 10:29–37), Jesus makes clear our responsibility to care for those in need. The Catholic Church teaches this responsibility in the following themes of Catholic Social Teaching.

Life and Dignity of the Human Person

All human life is sacred, and all people must be respected and valued over material goods. We are called to ask whether our actions as a society respect or threaten the life and dignity of the human person.

Call to Family, Community, and Participation

Participation in family and community is central to our faith and to a healthy society. Families must be supported so that people can participate in society, build a community spirit, and promote the well-being of all, especially those who are poor and vulnerable.

Rights and Responsibilities

Every person has a right to life as well as a right to those things required for human decency. As Catholics we have a responsibility to protect these basic human rights in order to achieve a healthy society.

Option for the Poor and Vulnerable

In our world many people are very rich while at the same time many are extremely poor. As Catholics we are called to pay special attention to the needs of those who are poor by defending and promoting their dignity and by meeting their immediate material needs.

The Dignity of Work and the Rights of Workers

The basic rights of workers must be respected: the right to productive work, fair wages, and private property; and the right to organize, join unions, and pursue economic opportunity. Catholics believe that the economy is meant to serve people and that work is not merely a way to make a living but an important way in which we participate in God's creation.

Solidarity

Because God is our Father, we are all brothers and sisters with the responsibility to care for one another. Solidarity is the attitude that leads Christians to share spiritual and material goods. Solidarity unites rich and poor, weak and strong, and helps to make a society that recognizes that we all depend upon one another.

Care for God's Creation

God is the Creator of all people and all things, and he wants us to enjoy his creation. The responsibility to care for all God has made is a requirement of our faith.

Songs of Our Faith

Song of Love

Chorus

Thank you, Jesus, for helping me to see.
Thank you, God, for the heart you've given me.
Thank you, Spirit, for coming to me,
and for showing me how to sing your song of love.

Verse 1

I saw someone lonely by the road,
someone my age sadly all alone.
I shared my friendship, and we talked a while.
I gave my hand. Jesus gave back a smile.

(Sing Chorus)

Verse 2

I saw Jesus inside my heart,
making me God's own work of art.
If I spread my joy in life each day,
I can show my love for God's world in every way.

(Sing Chorus)

Verse 3

I saw Jesus in friends and family
by my side, sharing and supporting me.
I found my heart had room for everyone.
Thank you, Spirit, for what you have begun.

(Sing Chorus)

Lord, You Have the Words

Refrain

Lord, you have the words of
everlasting life.
Lord, you have the words of
everlasting life.

Verse 1

The law of the Lord is perfect,
refreshing the soul;
the Lord's rule is to be trusted, the
simple find wisdom.

Lord, you have the words of
everlasting life.

Verse 2

The fear of the Lord is holy,
abiding forever;
the decrees of the Lord are true,
all of them just.

Lord, you have the words of
everlasting life.

Verse 3

The precepts of the Lord are right;
they gladden the heart;
the command of the Lord is clear,
giving light to the eye.

Lord, you have the words of
everlasting life.

Verse 4

They are worth more than gold,
than the finest gold,
sweeter than honey, than honey
from the comb.

(Sing Refrain)

If (Si)

English Refrain

If today you hear the voice of God,
harden not your heart.
If today you hear the voice of God,
harden not your heart.

Verse 1

To the tiny wind and the voice of the
hurricane,
open up my heart.
To the child at play or the cry of
another's pain,
open up my heart.

(Sing English Refrain)

Verse 2

To the stranger's need, to the need of
my family,
open up my heart.
To the law's firm rule, to the prophets
who call to me,
open up my heart.

(Sing English Refrain)

Verse 3

A la tierna brisa asi como al huracán,
abreel corazón.
A la dulce voz de aquel niño
que juega,
abreel corazón.

Spanish Refrain

Si tú oyes hoy la voz de Dios,
abreel corazón.
Si tú oyes hoy la voz de Dios,
abreel corazón.

Verse 4

Al desconocido y los llantos de mi hogar,
abreel corazón.
A la dura ley, al profeta que me invita,
abreel corazón.

(Sing Spanish Refrain)

Lead Me, Guide Me

Refrain

Lead me, guide me, along the way,
For if you lead me, I cannot stray.
Lord, let me walk each day with thee.
Lead me, oh Lord, lead me.

Verse 1

I am weak and I need thy strength
and power
To help me over my weakest hour.
Help me through the darkness
thy face to see.
Lead me, oh Lord, lead me.

(Sing Refrain)

Verse 2

I am lost if you take your hand from me,
I am blind without thy Light to see.
Lord, just always let me thy servant be.
Lead me, oh Lord, lead me.

(Sing Refrain)

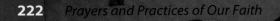

I Say "Yes," Lord/Digo "Sí," Señor

Verse 1

To the God who cannot die:
I say "Yes," my Lord.
(I say "Yes," my Lord.)
To the One who hears me cry:
I say "Yes," my Lord.
(I say "Yes," my Lord.)
To the God of the oppressed:
I say "Yes," my Lord.
(I say "Yes," my Lord.)
To the God of all justice:
I say "Yes," my Lord.
(I say "Yes," my Lord.)
I say "Yes," my Lord,
in all the good times,
through all the bad times,
I say "Yes," my Lord,
to every word you speak.

Verse 2

Like that of Job unceasingly:
Digo "Sí," Señor. (Digo "Sí," Señor.)
Like that of Maria wholeheartedly:
Digo "Sí," Señor. (Digo "Sí," Señor.)
Like that of David in a song:
Digo "Sí," Señor. (Digo "Sí," Señor.)
Like Israel, for you I long:
Digo "Sí," Señor. (Digo "Sí," Señor.)
Digo "Sí," Señor,
en tiempos malos, en tiempos buenos,
Digo "Sí," Señor,
a todo lo que hablas.

Shepherd Me, O God

Refrain

Shepherd me, O God,
beyond my wants,
beyond my fears
from death into life.

Verse 1

God is my shepherd,
so nothing shall I want,
I rest in the meadows
of faithfulness and love,
I walk by the quiet waters of peace.

(Sing Refrain)

Verse 2

Gently you raise me
and heal my weary soul,
you lead me by pathways of
righteousness and truth,
my spirit shall sing the
music of your name.

(Sing Refrain)

Verse 3

Though I should wander
the valley of death,
I fear no evil, for you are at my side,
your rod and your staff,
my comfort and my hope.

(Sing Refrain)

Verse 4

You have set me a banquet of love
in the face of hatred,
crowning me with love beyond my
power to hold.

(Sing Refrain)

Verse 5

Surely your kindness
and mercy follow me
all the days of my life;
I will dwell in the house of my God
forevermore.

(Sing Refrain Twice)

We Are Marching

Verse 1

We are marching in the light of God,
we are marching in the light of God.
We are marching in the light of God,
we are marching in the light of God, (in the light of God)
we are marching, marching, we are marching
oo
We are marching in the light of God, (in the light of God)
we are marching, marching, we are marching
oo
we are marching in the light of God.

Verse 2

We are singing in the light of God,
we are singing in the light of God.
We are singing in the light of God,
we are singing in the light of God, (in the light of God)
we are singing, singing, we are singing
oo
We are singing in the light of God,
(in the light of God)
we are singing, singing, we are singing
oo
we are singing in the light of God.

Open Your Ears, O Faithful People

Verse 1

Open your ears, O faithful people,
open your ears and hear God's Word.
Open your hearts, O royal priesthood,
God has come to you.

Refrain

God has spoken to the people, hallelujah!
God has spoken words of wisdom, hallelujah!
Torah ora, Torah ora, hallelujah!
Torah ora, Torah ora, hallelujah!

Verse 2

They who have ears to hear the message,
they who have ears, now let them hear;
they who would learn the way of wisdom,
let them hear God's Word.

(Sing Refrain)

Verse 3

Israel comes to greet the Savior,
Judah is glad to see his day;
from east and west the peoples travel,
God will show the way.

(Sing Refrain)

Give Your Gifts

Verse 1

My friends, there are different kinds of gifts
from the Spirit.
The Lord gives each one of us a call to share
if we hear it.
We all serve the same Lord
in our different ways,
and the Father will help us every day.

Refrain

Go and give your gifts to the world.
Go and give your gifts to the world.
I said give your gifts to the world.
Go and give your gifts to the world.

Verse 2

Like parts of one body we are
not the same,
but together,
for we are the body of Christ today
and forever.
Some can hear but not see.
Some can see but not hear.
But when we work together there's
nothing to fear.

(Sing Refrain)

Blessing Prayer

Refrain

May the road rise up to meet you.
May the wind be always with you.
May the sunshine warm you always,
'til we meet again.

Verse 1

May the rain fall softly on you.
May the hand of God uphold you.

(Sing Refrain)

Verse 2

Christ before you, Christ behind you.
Christ beneath you, Christ above you.

(Sing Refrain)

Verse 3

Christ to shield you, Christ be with you.
Christ be with you now and always.

(Sing Refrain)

Name _____ Date _____

Art Print 1 shows an illuminated Bible page. What was the benefit of adding beautiful artwork to these pages?

Copying the Bible

rom the time the Bible was first written until the invention of the printing press in the 15th century, copies of the Bible were written by hand. Saint Jerome worked with handwritten copies of the Bible in Hebrew and Greek and wrote his translation by hand in Latin. This Latin translation is called the **Vulgate** version of the Bible.

Writing a Bible took a long time, so not many copies existed. For about a thousand years, monks and nuns in **scriptoriums,** places where writing took place, made copies of the Bible by hand so that more people could use it for prayer and worship.

The monks and nuns wanted the Bibles to be easy to read, so they developed a clear kind of handwriting similar to ours today. To make the Bibles beautiful, they "illuminated" them. This meant that they added large, colorful letters and pictures of plants, animals, and scenes from everyday life.

Illuminated Bible

Sketch two pictures you would include if you illuminated a Bible.

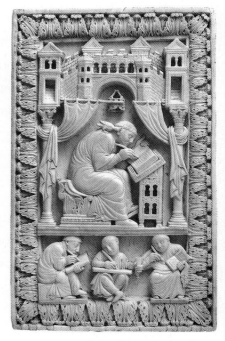

Saint Gregory the Great
and three scribes,
German ivory carving

www.findinggod.com

Grade 6 • Unit 1 • Session 1 • **229**

Name _____   Date _____

Art Print 2 shows Adam and Eve being expelled from the Garden of Eden.
What can we learn about our own faith from the story of Adam and Eve?

The Second Story of Creation

Although this story appears after the first Creation story in Genesis, it was actually written long before the Jews became exiles in Babylon. It was probably written while David and then his son Solomon reigned as kings of Israel.

> God created man and woman and put them in a garden to care for it. Together, man and woman—Adam and Eve—were to share equally and care for the earth as God does. They were allowed to eat the fruit from any tree in the garden except for one, from which God had forbidden them to eat. When they were tempted and ate the fruit from the forbidden tree, God made them leave the garden.
>
> *adapted from Genesis 2:4—3:24*

This passage highlights the importance of stewardship. We all have a responsibility to care for God's creation. This story also shows God's love. God still showed Adam and Eve his love and mercy, despite their disobedience.

Mercy and Love

Write a prayer thanking God for his mercy and love.

_____

_____

_____

Reading God's Word

What are humans that you are mindful of them,
  mere mortals that you care for them?
Yet you have made them little less than a god,
  crowned them with glory and honor.
You have given them rule over the works of your hands,
  put all things at their feet[.]

Psalm 8:5–7

Name _____   Date _____

Art Print 3 shows an interpretation of Noah building his ark.
Why is God's covenant with Noah important in building our faith today?

God Chooses Noah

After Adam and Eve left the Garden of Eden,
the world became a cruel and greedy place.
God chose one family who showed love, trust,
and obedience—Noah and his family. God told
them to build a huge ark and put two of every
creature on it. Even though people laughed,
Noah and his family obeyed. The rains came.
Noah's family and the animals got on the ark.
For 40 days and nights, the rain flooded the
world. Weeks later the ark rested on land.
Noah and his family survived.

adapted from Genesis 6:5—9:17

God's Promise

To help Noah, God put a rainbow in the sky as a sign of hope. God promised
he would never again send such a flood. When two people make an agreement
today, sometimes they sign it. The rainbow was God's signature. Even after
the world turned evil, God made a commitment, or covenant, to keep his
promise and never give up on people.

Your Promise

List three promises you can make to God as your personal covenant with him.

1. _____

2. _____

3. _____

Link to Liturgy

In the Penitential Act at Mass, we reflect on our sins and ask for God's
mercy. We pray "Lord have mercy" to praise God for his great mercy.

Name _____ Date _____

Art Print 4 shows an interpretation of a traditional Jewish dance, the hora. Why are the traditions of our ancestors important? How can these help us grow our faith?

The Chosen People

Because Abraham was willing to obey God, he promised that Abraham would be the father of not only Isaac, but of an entire nation of people.

When God made a covenant with Abraham, he started a new chapter in the story of our relationship with God. Ever since God's covenant with Abraham, Abraham's descendants have been known as God's **Chosen People.** God's Chosen People were given a mission to help other people learn about and trust God. In each generation God calls people to know him in a special way.

Jesus was a descendant of Abraham's. Through Jesus we can be God's people. Just as Abraham knew God, trusted him, and carried out his plans, we can too.

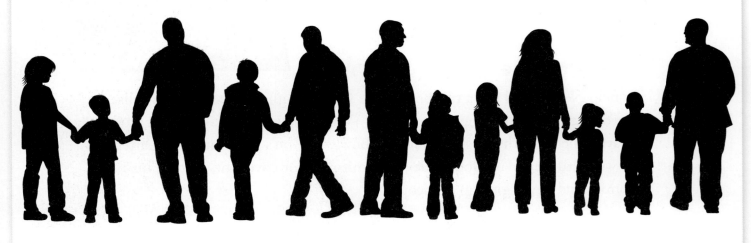

God's People

On a separate sheet of paper, list how we are connected to Abraham and Sarah. Explain what being God's Chosen People means to you. What are the rights and responsibilities of the Chosen People? Share your list with a partner.

Link to Liturgy

Catholics have customs that tell the world that we are God's people. One custom is the Sign of the Cross. When we pray the Sign of the Cross, we pray in the name of the Father, the Son, and the Holy Spirit. We do this a number of times at Mass.

Name _____ Date _____

Art Print 5 shows the symbols of the Evangelists. Why are these symbols, along with other Christian symbols, important to our relationship with Jesus?

Evangelists' Symbols

The Gospels, written by Matthew, Mark, Luke, and John, present the life, ministry, and miracles of Jesus. Like many aspects of the Church, the Gospel writers, or Evangelists, are represented by their own symbols. These symbols represent the theme of each Gospel writer.

Matthew is often depicted as a winged man to represent the humanness of Jesus. Mark's symbol, a winged lion, represents Christ the King. The winged ox for Luke is symbolic of Jesus Christ as a priest and as a man of sacrifice. John's symbol is an eagle. This is a symbol for Jesus' divine nature. When you enter church, look for these and other symbols as reminders of your faith.

Church Symbols

Select and draw a Christian symbol in the box.
Write what you think it means.

_____

_____

Name _____ Date _____

Art Print 6 shows an image of Joseph, Jacob's son. How can our own heritage help us grow in faith?

Jesus, Descendant of Jacob's

Jesus descended from a long line of men and women, including Jacob and King David. Jesus' ancestors were people who made mistakes and learned from them, just as we do.

Through the examples of Jesus and his ancestors, we can see that our choices and actions are part of God's plan. We all face difficult choices in life, and sometimes the choices we make hurt other people. Although we may not always understand God's plan, Jesus teaches us to trust the goodness and faithfulness of God.

Your Own Family Tree

On a separate sheet of paper, make a family tree. Include as many family members as you can recall. Then write a summary statement below, telling why it is important to know about your ancestors.

_____

_____

_____

_____

_____

Reading God's Word

And concerning the resurrection of the dead, have you not read what was said to you by God, "I am the God of Abraham, the God of Isaac, and the God of Jacob"? He is not the God of the dead but of the living.

Matthew 22:31–32

Name _____   Date _____

Art Print 7 shows an interpretation of a Seder celebration, which is part of Passover. Why are Passover and the Sabbath important to our Catholic faith?

Passover and the Sabbath

God told Moses that on a certain night an angel would travel over Egypt and kill the firstborn child in every family. If the Hebrew people followed God's instructions, their children would be spared. Moses told each family to kill a lamb and sprinkle its blood on the door of the house. If they did, the angel would pass over. God also instructed the Hebrews to eat a special meal.

adapted from Exodus 12:1–30

The meal and prayers offered on that night became a memorial known as the Passover. It was a memorial for the Hebrew people to help remember the night the angel passed over the Hebrew houses.

The **Sabbath** is a celebration we observe today. When God created the world, he rested on the seventh day. He commanded people to do the same. This day is called the Sabbath. Today Christians celebrate the Sabbath on Sunday when we recall Jesus' Resurrection.

Your Sunday

Sunday, the Sabbath, is an important day of holy celebration. Write two things you could do on the Sabbath to honor Jesus.

_____

_____

Link to Liturgy

Before receiving Holy Communion, we pray, "Lord, I am not worthy that you should enter under my roof, but only say the word and my soul shall be healed." With these words we are asking for God's help and forgiveness.

Name _____   Date _____

Art Print 8 shows a marble statue of Moses.
How do the Ten Commandments help us strengthen our relationship with God?

God Gives Moses the Ten Commandments

Moses went to Egypt to challenge the pharaoh for the Hebrew people. The pharaoh didn't cooperate and began a battle with God that could not be won. After finally releasing the Hebrew people, the pharaoh tried again to stop them. God crushed the pharaoh's army while Moses led the Hebrews across the sea.

When the Hebrews reached Mount Sinai, God gave Moses the Ten Commandments. God asked the Hebrews if they wanted to be his people. In response the people said yes and agreed to follow these commandments.

Jesus lived by the Ten Commandments and told others to do so. With God's help these basic instructions guide us to a strong relationship with God and with one another.

Moses Leads

Number the events in order.

_____ Moses and his people cross the sea.

_____ Moses challenges the pharaoh.

_____ God gives Moses the Ten Commandments on Mount Sinai.

_____ God crushes the pharaoh's army.

Reading God's Word

"Hear, O Israel! The LORD is our God, the LORD alone! Therefore, you shall love the LORD, your God, with all your heart, and with all your soul, and with all your strength."   *Deuteronomy 6:4–5*

Name _____ Date _____

Art Print 9 shows a scene from Ruth's story. How often do you consider all the consequences when making difficult choices?

Ruth's Choice

King David would not have been born had it not been for a woman named Ruth. She was a converted Moabite who married a Jewish man. When her husband died, she had a choice: remain in Moab with her relatives or go with her widowed mother-in-law, Naomi, to Israel. A widow relied on relatives for help, so Ruth chose to go with Naomi to take care of her.

Ruth set aside her own needs to care for her mother-in-law while they lived in Israel. She eventually married a distant relative of Naomi's named Boaz. Ruth became the great-grandmother of King David.

adapted from Ruth 1—4

Moral Decisions, Moral Consequences

David and Ruth made life-changing decisions with different consequences. David was arrogant and wanted to satisfy himself, costing Uriah his life. David was unable to make the right decision and lived with the consequences for the rest of his life. David's family life with Bathsheba was filled with conflict.

Ruth, however, placed the needs of Naomi first. Ruth's decision was good. Naomi had someone to care for her, and Ruth was remarried and started a family.

The Right Decision

Write an example of a time when you made the right decision.

_____

_____

_____

Name _____   Date _____

*Art Print 10 shows a stained-glass version of a Jesse Tree.
Why are Jesse Trees important in celebrating Advent?*

The Church Celebrates Advent

Throughout the Old Testament, the prophets share God's promise to
send the Messiah. In their messages, many hopeful, faithful people are
waiting for the Messiah. It would be a day of peace when "the wolf
will be a guest of the lamb. The leopard shall lie down with the kid.
The calf and young lion shall eat together with a little child to lead them."

adapted from Isaiah 11:6

During Advent we often see a **Jesse Tree** representing Jesus' family.
A Jesse Tree is decorated with symbols from the Bible. The
symbols help teach about the Messiah's ancestry. Symbols
for Adam and Eve, Abraham and Sarah, Isaac,
Noah, Moses, and King David are traditionally
seen. Mary and Joseph are included with
Jesus near the top of the tree. The
Jesse Tree is named after Jesse,
who was the father of King
David. Jesus' genealogy can be
traced back to Jesse.

A Family Jesse Tree

Brainstorm possible symbols
you would use to decorate a
Jesse Tree. On a separate sheet
of paper, make three drawings of
symbols from the list you wrote.

_____

_____

_____

_____

_____

Name _____   Date _____

Art Print 11 shows Jesus helping someone in need.
What qualities does Jesus portray in this image?

God's Presence in Jesus Christ

During his life Jesus had a special respect for the Temple at Jerusalem. For Jesus the Temple was not just a monument to God; it was his Father's house.

After the Resurrection, God's presence took on a new meaning. Christ himself became the ultimate priest, prophet, and king. His death on the cross became the final sacrifice. Jesus is the one mediator between God and us, his human family. Jesus is at the right hand of God the Father, where he intercedes for us. Jesus sends the Holy Spirit to gather the new People of God. We, as the People of God, are called the Church. We are the new Temple of the Holy Spirit. God no longer dwells in a stone house; he dwells within us, his people.

God's Presence Within Us

Write one quality, habit, and goal that allow you to accept God to dwell within you.

quality: _____

habit: _____

goal: _____

Reading God's Word

"Destroy this temple and in three days I will raise it up." Only after Jesus rose from the dead did his disciples recall and believe the Scripture and the words Jesus spoke.   *adapted from John 2:19,22*

Name _____ Date _____

Art Print 12 shows a shepherd leading his flock. How does this image remind you of Jesus?

Daily Experiences Make the Word Come Alive

Recall the story of Jacob, who worked for Laban for years to get permission to marry Laban's daughter. Jacob was a shepherd who diligently protected his sheep 24 hours a day. He would go hungry rather than eat one of them. In Genesis, Jacob says, "How often the scorching heat ravaged me by day, and the frost by night, while sleep fled from my eyes!"

adapted from *Genesis 31:38–40*

Jacob's life as a shepherd helps us understand God's relationship with us. Jacob sacrificed to protect his sheep as God cares for and protects us.

The LORD is my shepherd; there is nothing I lack. In green pastures you let me graze; to safe waters you lead me; you restore my strength. You guide me along the right path for the sake of your name. Even when I walk through a dark valley, I fear no harm for you are at my side; your rod and staff give me courage.

adapted from *Psalm 23:1–4*

Psalm 23 reminds us that God is there to protect us no matter what troubles we may encounter.

The Lord Is . . .

Complete the sentence with your image of God.

The Lord is _____

_____

_____

_____ .

Reading God's Word

Man may be merciful to his fellow man,
  but the LORD's mercy reaches all flesh,
Reproving, admonishing, teaching,
  as a shepherd guides his flock[.]

Sirach 18:11–12

Name _____ Date _____

Art Print 13 shows Jesus Christ with the apostles.
What do you think Jesus is telling Peter in the Art Print?

The Beginning of the Church

After Jesus was **crucified,** he was raised from the dead and appeared to his followers. He instructed his followers to wait for the Holy Spirit, who would come and help them continue to live as followers of Jesus Christ.

Peter explained how the Holy Spirit came to the disciples and reminds people of the words of the prophet Joel. "God would pour out his Spirit on all. Your sons and daughters shall prophesy, your old men shall see dreams, your young men shall see visions."

Peter proclaimed Jesus as the Messiah who fulfilled many prophesies of the Old Testament. Peter said, "God raised Jesus from the dead, as the Scriptures foretold. Jesus now sits at the right hand of God."

When the crowd heard Peter's explanation, many asked what they could do. Peter said "repent, be baptized, and receive forgiveness of your sins." About 3,000 Jews were baptized. All believed that Jesus was the Messiah. They formed the early Church.

adapted from Acts of the Apostles 2:1–41

About Jesus

Write three things Peter said about Jesus.

_____

_____

_____

Link to Liturgy

At Mass the priest or deacon tells us to glorify the Lord by our lives. Our response confirms that we will proclaim what we have learned in the readings and received in the Eucharist.

Art Print 14 shows Paul preaching. What was at the heart of Paul's message?

Paul Speaks of Love and Unity

The prophet Jeremiah witnessed the exile of the Jewish people in 587 B.C. His life was dedicated to having people commit themselves to God. Jeremiah's last words to the people were of hope, not despair. He repeated God's promise to make a new covenant with the people.

I will place my law within them, and write it upon their hearts;
I will be their God, and they shall be my people.   *Jeremiah 31:33*

In Paul's letters to the early Church, we see Jeremiah's hopes fulfilled. In his hope-filled letters from prison, Paul wrote to the Ephesians that he was convinced the Church would continue to cooperate with the Holy Spirit in building God's family.

Paul saw Christians making a difference in the world through acts of humility, gentleness, patience, and love. He encouraged Christians to treat one another with love as they learned from Jesus and the apostles.

Paul taught that all members of God's family are united in Christ. They discovered the law of God written upon their hearts and were all part of one body with Jesus Christ.
adapted from Ephesians 4:1–6,15–16

Christian Qualities

Write how you show the following qualities.

humility: _____

_____

patience: _____

_____

Name _____ Date _____

Art Print 15 depicts the three Wise Men.
What is their importance to the Christmas season?

The Church Celebrates the Christmas Season

During the Christmas season, we learn about the beginning of Jesus' life—his birth, Holy Family, baptism, and the visit of the Magi, or the Epiphany.

Epiphany means "revelation." This feast celebrates the announcement of Jesus' birth and the arrival of the Magi. The Magi could not call on a phone, send an e-mail or text message, or see the news on TV. The Magi, being astronomers, relied on a bright star to learn of the birth of a king.

According to tradition the Magi, named Caspar, Melchior, and Balthazar, were the first visitors to acknowledge Jesus as king. They came to worship him and bear gifts. The Magi's long journey is a symbol of our own journey through life, seeking Jesus. The presentation of Jesus to the Magi reminds us that Jesus' birth is important to the whole world.

Guiding Us

The bright Christmas star guided the Magi. We all need a guide in our lives to help us do the right thing. Write ways that Jesus can guide you.

_____

_____

_____

_____

Name _____ Date _____

Art Print 16 shows a painting of the prophet Jeremiah.
What was the main message of the Old Testament prophets?

A Prophet's Challenge

God's prophets had a holy job, or ministry, to perform. God called them to intervene in societies that no longer followed his commandments.

Prophets often asked citizens and rulers to share wealth, food, and other necessities. This tradition of sharing is still an important mission in today's Church.

In ancient Jewish society, as well as today, such messages were not always well received. People ignored prophets who asked them to share, even though they knew the goods created by God were not meant for a few. Sometimes a ruler would throw a prophet in prison or out of the country, hoping to silence him. But the prophets kept delivering God's words. God called on them and gave them the wisdom and strength to act. One such prophet, Jeremiah, taught from 629 to 588 B.C., hoping people would renew their covenant with God.

A Prophecy for Today

Write what each message would be if God sent a prophet today to speak to your country, your neighborhood, and you personally.

To your country: _____

_____

_____

To your neighborhood: _____

_____

_____

To you: _____

_____

Name _____   Date _____

Art Print 17 is a lithograph of the prophet Isaiah.
Why are Isaiah's prophecies important to the Gospels of the New Testament?

Jesus and the Prophecies of Old

The Gospel of Matthew contains many references to the prophetic books of the Old Testament, especially Isaiah. Matthew was a Jew and would have been quite familiar with the Old Testament prophecies. He was talking mostly to Jews, and he wanted to use their own Scriptures to prove how Jesus had fulfilled prophecies concerning the Messiah.

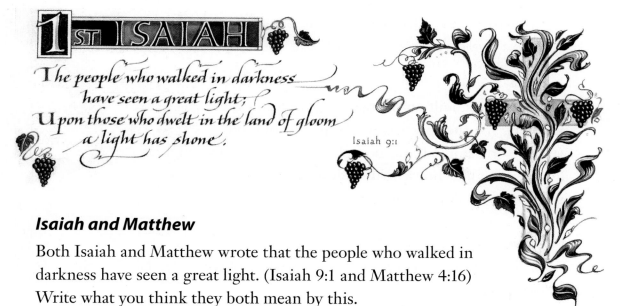

1st ISAIAH

The people who walked in darkness have seen a great light; Upon those who dwelt in the land of gloom a light has shone.

Isaiah 9:1

Isaiah and Matthew

Both Isaiah and Matthew wrote that the people who walked in darkness have seen a great light. (Isaiah 9:1 and Matthew 4:16) Write what you think they both mean by this.

_____

_____

_____

Did You Know?

The Book of Isaiah was written by different writers in three times and places. Chapters 1–39 were written between 738 and 700 B.C., when Judah was a kingdom and had been invaded by the Assyrians. Chapters 40–55 were written while the Jewish people were in exile. Chapters 56–66 were written after the people returned to Jerusalem from exile. The returning people felt hopeless because their kingdom was gone. The prophet called them to continue to believe in God, who had rescued them from Babylon.

Name _____   Date _____

Art Print 18 shows an image of St. Peter's Church in France.
What are the keystones of the Catholic Church?

The Stone That Holds Everything Together

The writer of Ephesians understood the importance of a strong foundation for the Church. The apostles and prophets are the foundation of the household of God, and Jesus is the keystone. A keystone is the stone in the center of an arch that holds it together.

> Through him the whole structure is held together and grows into a temple sacred in the Lord; in him you also are being built together into a dwelling place of God in the Spirit.
>
> *Ephesians 2:21–22*

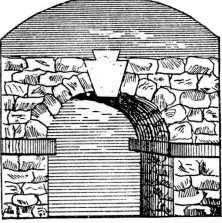

Keystone

The Church is built on the teachings of Jesus, the prophets, and the apostles. As the people of God, we are living stones in his household. Jesus holds us all together. This household made of living stones is a sign of God's presence in the world.

Your Keystone

Write an example of a person you know who holds other people together.

_____

_____

_____

_____

Reading God's Word

Come to him, a living stone, rejected by human beings but chosen and precious in the sight of God, and, like living stones, let yourselves be built into a spiritual house to be a holy priesthood to offer spiritual sacrifices acceptable to God through Jesus Christ.

1 Peter 2:4–5

Name _____ Date _____

Art Print 19 is a mosaic of a disciple curing a blind man.
How does this image connect to the Sacraments of Healing?

Jesus Sends Forth Healers

The Book of Isaiah has words of healing for those longing
for God in their lives.

> Then will the eyes of the blind be opened,
>   the ears of the deaf be cleared;
> Then the lame will leap like a stag,
>   then the tongue of the dumb will sing.   *Isaiah 35:5–6*

Jesus fulfilled this prophecy by proclaiming the good news of
God's kingdom. He gathered his apostles and gave them authority
to heal the sick. The disciples performed miracles in Jesus' name.

In Jesus' time those who were ill were shamefully kept apart
from society and considered unclean. Jesus' ministry of spiritual
and social healing cured physical ills and restored the dignity
everyone is granted by God.

The Church Celebrates Healing

Jesus continues to heal through the Church, calling upon
the Holy Spirit to pray for healing. The Holy Spirit gives
gifts for healing the body and spirit in the Sacraments of
Healing—the Anointing of the Sick and Reconciliation.

Be a Healer

Write an example of how you can be a healer.

_____

_____

_____

Reading God's Word

I come to gather nations of every language;
they shall come and see my glory.   *Isaiah 66:18*

Name _____   Date _____

Art Print 20 shows an interpretation of Gethsemane, where Jesus prayed after the Last Supper. Why is prayer important to Lent and Holy Week?

The Church Celebrates Lent and Holy Week

During the Lenten season, we prepare ourselves to observe the Death and Resurrection of Jesus. We remember the great sacrifice Jesus made by dying on the cross. Lent is a time to pray more often, make sacrifices such as fasting, and give to people in need. Through these acts we acknowledge relying on God. Receiving the Sacrament of Reconciliation during Lent gives us healing and strength.

When Jesus faced difficult decisions, he prayed. Near the end of his life after the Last Supper, Jesus went to the Garden of Gethsemane to pray. He felt great sorrow as he chose to bear our sins and die on the cross. Jesus put his will aside to obey his Father's will.

People seek Jesus today because of his great love. When you face difficult decisions, follow Jesus' example by praying for the strength to follow God's will.

Lenten Acts

Draw lines to match each Lenten promise with an act you can do.

1. pray
2. fast
3. help others

a. Have a meatless meal.
b. Donate to a food bank.
c. Reflect on a Bible passage.

Name _____ Date _____

Art Print 21 is a painting of Saint Thérèse of Lisieux. Why is she a great example of how we can show our appreciation for God every day?

A Young Woman Who Listened to God

Thérèse of Lisieux was born in 1873 in France. She wanted to join the Carmelite convent as her older sisters had, but the head of the convent did not think Thérèse was ready for the strict and rigorous convent life. Thérèse persisted to pursue her dreams of doing great things for God.

At age 14 she went on a pilgrimage to Rome with her father. There she saw a chance to join the convent. Even though they were forbidden to speak to the pope, she ran up to him and begged him to let her enter the Carmelite Order.

Although permission was not granted, a Church official noticed her courage and urged the head of the convent to admit her. At age 15 Thérèse entered the convent.

Thérèse showed her love for God by making small sacrifices every day and was constantly aware of God's presence in her life.

The Little Way

Write examples of small things you can do to show love for God and others.

Thérèse of Lisieux in July 1896

_____

_____

_____

Reading God's Word

Hear, O Israel! The LORD is our God, the LORD alone! Therefore, you shall love the LORD, your God, with all your heart, and with all your soul, and with all your strength.   *Deuteronomy 6:4–5*

Name _____ Date _____

Art Print 22 depicts an interpretation of the Wedding at Cana.
Why is the Sacrament of Matrimony such an important spiritual celebration?

Marriage: A Holy Calling

In the Sacrament of Matrimony, a woman and a man are called by the Holy Spirit into a marriage covenant with God and with each other. They make this commitment in a celebration before a priest, a deacon, or an authorized witness of the Church.

A husband and wife are called to holiness through their Baptism. They receive the grace to love each other and their children, whom they care for and educate in the faith. Their relationship reflects the union between Christ and the Church. They live as one couple, physically and emotionally.

Chastity unites a couple spiritually: "I promise to be true to you in good times and bad, in sickness and in health. I will love you and honor you all the days of my life."

They commit to being a faithful couple for life, witnessing to God's faithfulness and infinite love, and accepting children. A child, created in God's likeness, must be treated as a human being from the moment of conception.

Matrimony Interview

Write three questions to ask a relative about his or her wedding ceremony.

1. _____

2. _____

3. _____

Link to Liturgy

During the celebration of the Sacrament of Matrimony, rings are exchanged as symbols of deep faith, peace, and the promise of unconditional love and fidelity toward each other.

Name _____   Date _____

Art Print 23 is a painting of human life coexisting with nature.
Why is it our responsibility to care for God's creation?

Gospel of Life: A Letter to the Church

We have a special relationship with the natural world and find joy in its beauty and diversity. We depend on nature for survival and harness its natural resources for social benefits. All people must share the goods of the earth and have enough to meet basic needs. It is important to appreciate and have a healthy relationship with the environment we live in.

In 1995 Pope John Paul II wrote an **encyclical**, a letter of instruction to the Church, called *The Gospel of Life.* The message teaches that all life is a sacred gift from God. As God's people we have the responsibility to care for the environment in which we live. We are entrusted to share in God's lordship over the world by defending and promoting life and showing reverence and love for it. Our calling, to protect and preserve God's creation, is not only for the present, but also for future generations.

Care for the Environment

Write two ways you can preserve the environment for future generations.

_____

_____

Link to Liturgy

At the end of the Liturgy of the Word, we pray the Prayer of the Faithful for the needs of the world, the Church, and the parish community. After each prayer we respond "Lord, hear our prayer" or similar words.

Name _____   Date _____

Art Print 24 shows Saint Patrick. Why are the saints important role models in our faith?

The Slave Becomes the Servant

Saint Patrick knew what it was like to lose his rights as a person. The son of a military officer in Britain, he was captured by pirates and enslaved in Ireland. For six years he worked as a shepherd, suffering from hunger, cold, and loneliness. He never lost his faith and prayed to God daily.

Eventually Patrick escaped and returned home. Once free, he became a priest to help others achieve the same rights he once lost.

After several years in parish ministry, Patrick was ordained a bishop. He answered God's call to return to Ireland. He returned and preached to the Celtic tribes, introducing them to Christianity. He changed the social life of Ireland by establishing monasteries, convents, and parishes, and by adapting pagan celebrations to Christian feasts.

Patrick forgave those who had enslaved him and helped establish systems and practices that supported people's dignity and freedom. His feast day is March 17.

Patrick Prays

Write a prayer Patrick may have said at these times in his life.

As a slave: _____

_____

As a bishop: _____

_____

Name _____ Date _____

Art Print 25 is a visual reminder of all the gifts God has given us. What are some of these gifts, and why are these important to remember at Easter?

The Church Celebrates Easter

We celebrate the Resurrection and Ascension of Jesus at Easter. Through these acts, Jesus brings us the gift of Salvation and the knowledge that we have been saved.

The Church gathers on Holy Saturday evening to celebrate the Easter Vigil. This is the beginning of Easter. The Easter Vigil has four parts: Service of Light, Liturgy of the Word, Liturgy of Baptism, and Liturgy of the Eucharist.

During the Liturgy of the Word, the story of God's love for us is proclaimed in the readings of the Old and New Testaments. The Old Testament readings recall the history of Salvation, beginning with creation and continuing with God's people who were waiting for thousands of years for the Savior to come. Salvation is the gift of new life in Jesus and our challenge to accept this gift by caring for God's creation and one another.

Interviewing Our Faith

Choose an Old Testament figure. Write what you would say to or ask this person who waited faithfully for Jesus to come.

_____

_____

_____

_____

Glossary

A

Abba an informal name for *father* in Aramaic, the language Jesus spoke. It is like *dad* in English. When Jesus spoke to God the Father, he called him "Abba." [Abba]

absolution the forgiveness we receive from God through the priest in the Sacrament of Penance and Reconciliation [absolución]

Advent the four weeks before Christmas. It is a time of joyful preparation for the celebration of the Incarnation, Jesus' birth as our Savior, and a time for anticipating the coming of Jesus Christ at the end of time. [Adviento]

Advocate Jesus' name for the Holy Spirit. The Holy Spirit comforts us, speaks for us in difficult times, and makes Jesus present to us. [Abogado]

Alleluia a prayer of praise to God. It is usually sung as the Gospel Acclamation before the proclamation of the Gospel Reading at Mass except during Lent. [Aleluya]

All Saints Day November 1, the day on which the Church honors all who have died and now live with God as saints in Heaven. This group includes those who are officially recognized as saints as well as many unknown people who after a good life have died and now live in God's presence. The feast celebrates our union with those who have gone before us and points to our ultimate goal of union with God. [Día de Todos los Santos]

All Souls Day November 2, the day on which the Church prays that all friends of God who have died may rest in peace. Those who have died may need purification in Purgatory before living fully in God's presence. Our prayers and good works can help them in this process. Along with All Saints Day, this feast reminds us that all who love God, living and dead, are united in living communion with Jesus Christ and with one another. [Día de los Fieles Difuntos]

almsgiving the practice of giving money to those in need as an act of love [limosna, dar]

altar the table in the church on which the priest celebrates Mass, where the sacrifice of Christ on the cross is made present in the Sacrament of the Eucharist. The altar represents two aspects of the mystery of the Eucharist. It is the place where Jesus Christ offers himself for our sins and where he gives us himself as our food for eternal life. [altar]

ambo a raised stand from which a person reads the Word of God during Mass [ambón]

Amen the Hebrew word used to conclude Jewish and Christian prayers. It means "This is true," "So be it," or "Let it be so." We end prayers with *Amen* to show that we mean what we have just said. [Amén]

angel a spiritual creature who worships God in Heaven. Angels serve God as messengers. They tell us of God's plans for our Salvation. [ángel]

Angelus a Catholic devotion recited three times a day—morning, noon, and evening. The devotion reflects on the mystery of the Incarnation—the coming of the angel to Mary, her acceptance of the invitation to be the mother of Jesus, and the Word made flesh. [Ángelus]

Annunciation the announcement to Mary by the angel Gabriel that God had chosen her to be the mother of Jesus. When Mary agreed, the Son of God became man in her. The Feast of the Annunciation is celebrated on March 25, nine months before Christmas. [Anunciación]

Anointing of the Sick one of the seven sacraments. In this sacrament a sick person is anointed with holy oil and receives the strength, peace, and courage to overcome the difficulties associated with illness. Through this sacrament Jesus brings the sick person spiritual healing and forgiveness of sins. If it is God's will, healing of the body is given as well. [Unción de los enfermos]

apostle one of twelve chosen men who accompanied Jesus in his ministry and were witnesses to the Resurrection. *Apostle* means "one sent." These were the men sent to preach the Gospel to the whole world. [apóstol]

Apostles' Creed a statement of Christian belief that developed out of a creed used in Baptism in Rome. The Apostles' Creed lists simple statements of belief in God the Father, Jesus Christ the Son, and the Holy Spirit. It is the basis for the profession of faith used in Baptism today. [Credo de los Apóstoles]

apostolic one of the four Marks of the Church. The Church is apostolic because it continues to hand on the teaching of the apostles through their successors, the bishops, in union with the successor of Saint Peter, the pope. [apostólico]

Ark of the Covenant the sacred box God commanded Moses to build (Exodus 25:10–16), made of acacia wood to hold the restored tablets of the Law [Arca de la alianza]

Ascension the entry of Jesus into God's presence in Heaven. In the Acts of the Apostles, it is written that Jesus, after his Resurrection, spent 40 days on earth, instructing his followers. He then returned to his Father in Heaven. [Ascensión]

Ash Wednesday the first day of Lent, on which we receive ashes on our foreheads. The ashes remind us to prepare for Easter by repenting and showing sorrow for the choices we make that offend God and hurt our relationships with others. [Miércoles de Ceniza]

assembly the People of God when they are gathered together to worship him [asamblea]

Assumption Mary's being taken, body and soul, into Heaven. Mary had a special relationship with her Son, Jesus, from the very beginning, when she conceived him. Catholics believe that because of this relationship, she enjoys a special participation in Jesus' Resurrection and has been taken into Heaven where she now lives with him. We celebrate this event in the Feast of the Assumption on August 15. [Asunción]

B

Baptism the first of the seven sacraments. Baptism frees us from Original Sin and is necessary for Salvation. Baptism gives us new life in Jesus Christ through the Holy Spirit. The celebration of Baptism consists of immersing a person in water while declaring that the person is baptized in the name of the Father, the Son, and the Holy Spirit. [Bautismo]

baptismal font The water vessel where the Sacrament of Baptism is celebrated. The baptismal font may be located in a separate baptistery, near the entrance of the church, or in the midst of the community. [pila bautismal]

basic rights the human rights a government should protect, such as religious liberty, personal freedom, access to necessary information, right to life, and protection from terror and torture. [derechos humanos básicos]

basilica the term used to designate a certain church of historical significance in a local area. Major basilicas are in Rome and are designated churches of ancient origin that serve as places of pilgrimage. Minor basilicas are designated churches that have historical or devotional importance in local areas throughout the world. [basílica]

Beatitudes the teachings of Jesus in the Sermon on the Mount in Matthew's Gospel. The Beatitudes are eight ways of living the Christian life. They are the fulfillment of the commandments given to Moses. These teachings present the way to true happiness. [Bienaventuranzas]

Bible the collection of books containing the truths of God's revelation to us. These writings were inspired by the Holy Spirit and written by human beings. The Bible is made up of the 46 books in the Old Testament and 27 books in the New Testament. [Biblia]

bishop a man who has received the fullness of Holy Orders. As a successor to the original apostles, he takes care of the Church and is a principal teacher in it. [obispo]

Blessed Sacrament the Eucharist that has been consecrated by the priest at Mass. It is kept in the tabernacle to adore and to be taken to those who are sick. [Santísimo Sacramento]

blessing a prayer that calls for God's power and care upon some person, place, thing, or special activity [bendición]

Body and Blood of Christ the Bread and Wine that have been consecrated by the priest at Mass. In the Sacrament of the Eucharist, all of the risen Lord Jesus Christ—body, blood, soul, and divinity—is present in the form of Bread and Wine. [Cuerpo y Sangre de Cristo]

Bread of Life a title that Jesus gives himself in John 6:33–35. Jesus is the Bread of the Eucharist. He becomes spiritual food for the faithful. [pan de vida]

C

Canaan the name of the land between Syria and Egypt in which the Israelites settled [Caná]

canonize to declare that a Christian who has died is already a saint in Heaven and may be looked to as a model of Christian life who may intercede for us [canonizar]

capital sins those sins that can lead us to more serious sin. They are pride, covetousness, envy, anger, gluttony, lust, and sloth. [pecados capitales]

cast lots to throw down small stones or pebbles called lots to help determine a decision needing divine guidance. Lots were cast to choose the disciple to replace Judas in Acts of the Apostles 1:23–26. Roman soldiers also cast lots to divide Jesus' clothing among them as in John 19:24. [echar a suertes]

catechumen a person being formed in the Christian life through instruction and by the example of the parish community. Through conversion and maturity of faith, a catechumen is preparing to be welcomed into the Church at Easter through the Sacraments of Baptism, Confirmation, and the Eucharist. [catecúmeno]

catholic one of the four Marks of the Church. The Church is catholic because Jesus is fully present in it and because Jesus has given the Church to the whole world. It is universal. [católico]

celebrant a bishop or priest who leads the people in praying the Mass. A deacon who baptizes or witnesses a marriage is also a celebrant. [celebrante]

celebrate worshiping, praising, and thanking God for what he has done for us with prayers and songs, especially in the celebration of the Eucharist. [celebrar]

character a permanent spiritual mark. Character shows that a person has a new relationship with Jesus and a special standing in the Church. Baptism, Confirmation, and Holy Orders each have a specific permanent character and therefore may be received only once. [carácter]

charity a virtue given to us by God that helps us love God above all things and our neighbor as ourselves [caridad]

chastity the integration of our physical sexuality with our spiritual nature. Chastity helps us to be completely human, able to give to others our whole life and love. All people, married and single, are called to practice chastity. [castidad]

chasuble the visible liturgical vestment worn by the bishop or priest at Mass. The newly ordained priest receives a chasuble as part of the ordination ritual. [casulla]

Chosen People the people set apart by God to have a special relationship with him. God first formed a Chosen People when he made a covenant, or solemn agreement, with Abraham. He reaffirmed the Covenant through Moses at Mount Sinai. The covenant is fulfilled in Jesus and his Church. [pueblo elegido]

Chrism a perfumed oil, consecrated by a bishop, that is used in the Sacraments of Baptism, Confirmation, and Holy Orders. Anointing with Chrism signifies the call of the baptized to the threefold ministry of priest, prophet, and king. [crisma]

Christ a title that means "anointed with oil." It is from a Greek word that means the same thing as the Hebrew word *Messiah*, or "anointed." It is the name given to Jesus after the Resurrection when he completed his mission as priest, prophet, and king. [Cristo]

Christian the name given to all those who have been anointed through the gift of the Holy Spirit in Baptism and have become followers of Jesus Christ [cristiano]

Christmas the feast of the birth of Jesus (December 25) [Navidad]

Church the People of God throughout the whole world, or diocese (the local Church), or the Assembly of those called together to worship God. The Church is one, holy, catholic, and apostolic. [Iglesia]

clergy those men who are set apart as sacred ministers to serve the Church through Holy Orders [clero]

commandment a standard, or rule, for living as God wants us to live. Jesus summarized all the commandments into two: love God and love your neighbor. [mandamiento]

communal prayer the worship of God together with others. The Liturgy of the Hours and the Mass are the main forms of communal prayer. [oración común]

Communion of Saints the unity of all, dead or living, who have been saved in Jesus Christ. The Communion of Saints is based on our one faith, and it is nourished by our participation in the Eucharist. [Comunión de los Santos]

community Christians who are gathered in the name of Jesus Christ to receive his grace and live according to his values. [comunidad]

compassion God's fundamental attitude toward his people. This is best seen in Jesus' reaching out to heal those in need. Acting with compassion and mercy toward those in need identifies a person as belonging to God. [compasión]

confession the act of telling our sins to a priest in the Sacrament of Penance and Reconciliation. The sacrament itself is sometimes referred to as confession. [confesión]

Confirmation the sacrament that completes the grace we receive in Baptism. It seals, or confirms, this grace through the seven Gifts of the Holy Spirit that we receive as part of Confirmation. This sacrament also makes us better able to participate in the worship and apostolic life of the Church. [Confirmación]

conscience the inner voice that helps each of us to judge the morality of our own actions. It guides us to follow God's law by doing good and avoiding evil. [conciencia]

consecration the making of a thing or a person to be special to God through a prayer or blessing. At Mass the words of the priest are a consecration of the bread and wine that become the Body and Blood of Christ. People or objects set apart for God in a special way are also consecrated. For example, churches and altars are consecrated for use in liturgy, and bishops are consecrated as they receive the fullness of the Sacrament of Holy Orders. [consagración]

contrition the sorrow we feel when we know that we have sinned, followed by the decision not to sin again. Perfect contrition arises from a love that loves God above all else. Imperfect contrition arises from other motives. Contrition is the most important act of the penitent preparing to celebrate the Sacrament of Penance and Reconciliation. [contrición]

conversion a radical or serious change of the whole life, away from sin and toward God. The call to change of heart is a key part of the preaching of Jesus. Throughout our entire lives, Jesus calls us to change in this way. [conversión]

Corporal Works of Mercy kind acts by which we help our neighbors with their everyday material needs. Corporal Works of Mercy include feeding the hungry, finding a home for the homeless, clothing the naked, visiting the sick and those in prison, giving alms to the poor, and burying the dead. [obras corporales de misericordia]

counsel one of the seven Gifts of the Holy Spirit. Counsel helps us to make correct choices in life through reflection, discernment, consultation, and advisement. [consejo]

covenant a solemn agreement between people or between people and God. God made covenants with humanity through agreements with Noah, Abraham, and Moses. These covenants offered Salvation. God's new and final covenant was established through Jesus' life, Death, Resurrection, and Ascension. *Testament* is another word for *covenant*. [alianza]

covet the excessive desire to possess something of value belonging to another person to the point of letting envy destroy the relationship [codiciar]

creation God's act of making everything that exists outside himself. Creation is everything that exists. God said that all of creation is good. [creación]

Creator God, who made everything that is and whom we can come to know through everything he created [Creador]

creed a brief summary of what people believe. The word *creed* comes from the Latin *credo*, "I believe." The Nicene Creed is the most important summary of Christian beliefs. [credo]

crosier the staff carried by a bishop that shows he cares for us in the same way that a shepherd cares for his sheep. It also reminds us that he represents Jesus, the Good Shepherd. [báculo]

crucified the way in which Jesus was put to death, nailed to a cross. As the crucified one, Jesus died for the sake of the world. [crucificado]

culture the collection of knowledge, belief, and behavior of a particular group of people. Culture expresses the shared attitudes, values, goals, and social practices of the group. To take root in a culture, the Gospel must be adapted to live in that culture as well as transform it. [cultura]

D

deacon a man ordained through the Sacrament of Holy Orders to the ministry of service in the Church. Deacons help the bishop and priests by serving in the various charitable practices of the Church. They help by proclaiming the Gospel and preaching and by assisting at the Liturgy of the Eucharist. Deacons also celebrate Baptism, bless marriages, and preside at funerals. [diácono]

detraction the act of talking about the faults and sins of another person to someone who has no reason to hear this and cannot help the person. Detraction damages the reputation of another person without any intent to help that person. [detracción]

diocese the members of the Church in a particular area, united in faith and the sacraments, and gathered under the leadership of a bishop [diócesis]

disciple a person who has accepted Jesus' message and tries to live as he did, sharing his mission, his suffering, and his joys [discípulo]

discipleship for Christians, the willingness to answer the call to follow Jesus. The call is received in Baptism, nourished in the Eucharist, and practiced in service to the world. [discipulado]

discrimination the act of mistreating other people because of how they look or act, or just because they are different [discriminación]

Dismissal the part of the Concluding Rites of the Mass in which the people are sent forth by the priest or deacon to do good works and praise and bless God [despedida]

Divine Praises a series of praises beginning with "Blessed be God," traditionally prayed at the end of the worship of the Blessed Sacrament in benediction [alabanzas de desagravio]

Divine Providence the guidance of God over all he has created. Divine Providence exercises care for all creation and guides it toward its final perfection. [Divina Providencia]

Doctor of the Church a man or a woman recognized as a model teacher of the Christian faith [Doctor de la Iglesia]

domestic church the Christian home, which is a community of grace and prayer and a school of human virtues and Christian charity [Iglesia doméstica]

doxology from two Greek words *doxa*, "glory," and *logos*, "word" or "saying." In the liturgy it is our way of giving praise to God for being who he is and for what he has done and will do. [doxología]

E

Easter the celebration of the bodily raising of Jesus Christ from the dead. Easter is the festival of our redemption and the central Christian feast, the one from which other feasts arise. [Pascua]

Eastern Catholic Churches a group of churches that developed in the Near East (in countries such as Lebanon) that are in union with the Roman Catholic Church but have their own liturgical, theological, and administrative traditions. They show the truly catholic nature of the Church, which takes root in many cultures. [Iglesias Católicas Orientales]

Easter Vigil the celebration of the first and greatest Christian feast, the Resurrection of Jesus. It occurs on the first Saturday evening after the first full moon of spring. During this night watch before Easter morning, catechumens are baptized, confirmed, and receive Eucharist for the first time. [Vigilia Pascual]

Emmanuel a Hebrew name from the Old Testament that means "God with us." In Matthew's Gospel, Jesus is called *Emmanuel*. [Emanuel]

encyclical a letter written by the pope and sent to the whole Church and sometimes to the whole world. It expresses Church teaching on some specific and important issue. [encíclica]

envy a feeling of resentment or sadness because someone has a quality, a talent, or a possession that we want. Envy is one of the seven capital sins, and it is contrary to the Tenth Commandment. [envidia]

Epiphany the day on which we celebrate the visit of the Magi to Jesus after his birth. This is the day that Jesus was revealed as the Savior of the whole world. [Epifanía]

epistle a letter written by Saint Paul or another leader to a group of Christians in the early Church. Twenty-one of the 27 books of the New Testament are epistles. The Second Reading at Mass on Sundays and holy days is always from one of these books. [epistola]

eternal life living happily with God in Heaven when we die in grace and friendship with him. Jesus calls all people to eternal life. [vida eterna]

Eucharist the sacrament in which we give thanks to God for giving us the consecrated Bread and Wine that become the Body and Blood of Jesus Christ. This sacrament brings us into union with Jesus Christ and his saving Death and Resurrection. [Eucaristía]

Eucharistic liturgy the public worship, held by the Church, in which the consecrated Bread and Wine become the Body and Blood of Jesus Christ. The Sunday celebration of the Eucharistic liturgy is at the heart of Church life. [liturgia eucarística]

Eucharistic Prayer during the Mass the liturgical expression of praise and thanksgiving for all that God has done in creation and in the Paschal Mystery (Christ's dying and rising from the dead for all) and through the Holy Spirit [Plegaria Eucarística]

euthanasia an action taken or omitted that purposely results in the death of a sick, disabled, or dying person. It is always gravely wrong and morally unacceptable. [eutanasia]

Evangelists the four men credited with writing the Gospels of Matthew, Mark, Luke, and John [evangelista]

evangelization the proclamation, or declaring by word and by example, of the good news about the Salvation we have received in Jesus Christ. Evangelization is a sharing of our faith with others, both those who do not know Jesus and those who are called to follow Jesus more closely. [evangelización]

examination of conscience the act of prayerfully thinking about what we have said or done in light of what the Gospel asks of us. We also think about how our actions may have hurt our relationship with God or with others. An examination of conscience is an important part of our preparing to celebrate the Sacrament of Penance and Reconciliation. [examen de conciencia]

Exile the period in the history of Israel between the destruction of Jerusalem in 587 B.C. and the return to Jerusalem in 537 B.C. During this time many of the Jewish people were forced to live in Babylon, far from home. [exilio]

Exodus God's liberation of the Hebrew people from slavery in Egypt and his leading them to the Promised Land [Éxodo]

F

faith a gift of God that helps us to believe in him. We profess our faith in the creed, celebrate it in the sacraments, live by it through our good conduct of loving God and our neighbor, and express it in prayer. [fe]

fasting limiting the amount we eat for a period of time to express sorrow for sin and to make ourselves more aware of God's action in our lives. Adults 18 years old and older fast on Ash Wednesday and Good Friday. The practice is also encouraged as a private devotion at other times of penitence. [ayuno]

fear of the Lord one of the seven Gifts of the Holy Spirit. This gift leads us to a sense of wonder and awe in the presence of God because we recognize his greatness. [temor de Dios]

Feast of the Holy Family celebrated on the Sunday that falls within the octave of Christmas, or, if no Sunday falls within the octave, on December 30. The feast celebrates the family of Jesus, Mary, and Joseph as a model for all Catholic families. [Fiesta de la Sagrada Familia]

forgiveness the willingness to be kind to those who have hurt us but have then shown that they are sorry. In the Lord's Prayer, we pray that since God will forgive us for our sins, we are able to forgive those who have hurt us. [perdón]

fortitude the strength to choose to do the right thing even when that is difficult. Fortitude is one of the four central human virtues, called the cardinal virtues, by which we guide our conduct through faith and the use of reason. It is also one of the Gifts of the Holy Spirit. [fortaleza]

free will the ability to choose to do good because God has made us like him. Our free will is what makes us truly human. Our exercise of free will to do good increases our freedom. Using free will to choose sin makes us slaves to sin. [libre albedrío]

Fruits of the Holy Spirit the demonstration through our actions that God is alive in us. Saint Paul lists the Fruits of the Holy Spirit in Galatians 5:22–23: love, joy, peace, patience, kindness, generosity, faithfulness, gentleness, and self-control. Church Tradition has added goodness, modesty, and chastity to make a total of 12. [frutos del Espíritu Santo]

G

Garden of Eden a garden created by God, filled with trees and lush vegetation, where God first placed Adam and Eve and from which they were later expelled [Jardín del Edén]

genuflect to show respect in church by touching a knee to the ground, especially before the Blessed Sacrament in the tabernacle [genuflexión, hacer la]

gestures the movements we make, such as the Sign of the Cross or bowing, to show our reverence during prayer [gestos]

gift of peace the peace that Jesus gives to us that flows from his relationship with his Father. This is the peace that the world cannot give, for it is the gift of Salvation that only Jesus can give. [don de la paz]

Gifts of the Holy Spirit the permanent willingness, given to us by the Holy Spirit, that makes it possible for us to do what God asks of us. The Gifts of the Holy Spirit are drawn from Isaiah 11:1–3. They include wisdom, understanding, counsel, fortitude, knowledge, and fear of the Lord. Church Tradition has added piety to make a total of seven. [dones del Espíritu Santo]

God the Father, Son, and Holy Spirit, one God in three distinct Persons. God created all that exists. He is the source of Salvation, and he is truth and love. [Dios]

godparent a witness to Baptism who assumes the responsibility for helping the baptized person along the road of Christian life [padrino/madrina de Bautismo]

Gospel the good news of God's mercy and love that we experience by hearing the story of Jesus' life, Death, and Resurrection. The story is passed on in the teaching ministry of the Church as the source of all truth and right living. It is presented to us in four books in the New Testament: the Gospels of Matthew, Mark, Luke, and John. [Evangelio]

grace the gift from God given to us without our meriting it. Sanctifying grace fills us with God's life and makes it possible for us always to be his friends. Grace is the Holy Spirit alive in us, helping us to live our Christian vocation. Grace helps us to live as God wants us to live. [gracia]

Great Commandment Jesus' commandment that we are to love both God and our neighbor as we love ourselves. Jesus tells us that this commandment sums up everything taught in the Old Testament. [Mandamiento Mayor, el]

guardian angel the angel who has been appointed to protect, pray for, and help a person live a holy life [ángel de la guarda]

H

habit the distinctive clothing worn by members of religious orders. It is a sign of the religious life and a witness to poverty. [hábito]

Heaven union with God the Father, Son, and Holy Spirit in life and love that never ends. Heaven is a state of complete happiness and the goal of the deepest wishes of the human heart. [cielo]

Hebrews the descendants of Abraham, Isaac, and Jacob, who were enslaved in Egypt. God helped Moses lead the Hebrews out of slavery. (*See* Israelites.) [hebreos]

Hell a life of total separation from God forever. In his infinite love for us, God can only desire our Salvation. Hell is the result of the free choice of a person to reject God's love and forgiveness once and for all. [infierno]

holiness the fullness of Christian life and love. All people are called to holiness, which is made possible by cooperating with God's grace to do his will. As we do God's will, we are transformed more and more into the image of the Son, Jesus Christ. [santidad]

holy one of the four Marks of the Church. It is the kind of life we live when we share in the life of God, who is all holiness. The Church is holy because it is united with Jesus Christ. [santa]

Holy Communion the consecrated Bread and Wine that we receive at Mass, which is the Body and Blood of Jesus Christ. It brings us into union with Jesus and his saving Death and Resurrection. [Sagrada Comunión]

Holy Days of Obligation the principal feast days, other than Sundays, of the Church. On Holy Days of Obligation, we celebrate the great things that God has done for us through Jesus and the saints. Catholics are obliged to participate in the Eucharist on these days, just as we are on Sundays. [días de precepto]

Holy Family the family of Jesus as he grew up in Nazareth. It included Jesus; his mother, Mary; and his foster father, Joseph. [Sagrada Familia]

Holy of Holies the holiest part of the Temple in Jerusalem. The high priest entered this part of the Temple once a year to address God and ask his forgiveness for the sins of the people. [Sanctasanctórum]

Holy Orders the sacrament through which the mission given by Jesus to his apostles continues in the Church. The sacrament has three degrees: deacon, priest, and bishop. Through the laying on of hands in the Sacrament of Holy Orders, men receive a permanent sacramental mark that calls them to minister to the Church. [sacramento del Orden]

Holy Spirit the third Person of the Trinity, who is sent to us as our helper and, through Baptism and Confirmation, fills us with God's life. Together with the Father and the Son, the Holy Spirit brings the divine plan of Salvation to completion. [Espíritu Santo]

Holy Thursday the Thursday of Holy Week on which the Mass of the Lord's Supper is celebrated, commemorating the institution of the Eucharist. The season of Lent ends with the celebration of this Mass. [Jueves Santo]

holy water water that has been blessed and is used as a sacramental to remind us of our Baptism [agua bendita]

Holy Week the celebration of the events surrounding Jesus' establishment of the Eucharist, his suffering, Death, and Resurrection. Holy Week commemorates Jesus' triumphal entry into Jerusalem on Palm Sunday, the gift of himself in the Eucharist on Holy Thursday, his Death on Good Friday, and his Resurrection at the Easter Vigil on Holy Saturday. [Semana Santa]

Homily the explanation by a bishop, a priest, or a deacon of the Word of God in the liturgy. The Homily relates the Word of God to our life as Christians today. [homilía]

honor giving God or a person the respect that they are owed. God is given this respect as our Creator and Redeemer. All people are worthy of respect as children of God. [honrar]

hope the confidence that God will always be with us, make us happy now and forever, and help us to live so that we will be with him forever [esperanza]

human condition the general state of humankind. While the human family is created in the image and likeness of God, it is also wounded by sin and often rejects the grace won by Jesus Christ. So while called by God to the highest good, too often human behavior leads to personal and social destruction. [condición humana]

I

idolatry in the Bible, the pagan worship of physical images given adoration as gods. For Christians today idolatry occurs whenever someone honors and reveres something in place of God. This can mean giving honor to power, pleasure, race, ancestors, or money over that which is owed to God. [idolatría]

Incarnation the Son of God, Jesus, being born as a full human being in order to save us. The Son of God, the second Person of the Trinity, is both true God and true man. [Encarnación]

indulgence a lessening of the punishment due for sins that have been forgiven. Indulgences move us toward our final purification, when we will live with God forever. [indulgencia]

inspired influenced by the Holy Spirit. The human authors of Scripture were influenced by the Holy Spirit. The creative inspiration of the Holy Spirit made sure that the Scripture was written according to the truth God wants us to know for our Salvation. [inspirado]

interpretation an explanation of the words of Scripture, combining human knowledge and the teaching office of the Church under the guidance of the Holy Spirit [interpretación]

Islam the third great religion, along with Judaism and Christianity, professing belief in one God. *Islam* means "submission" to that one God. [islamismo]

Israelites the descendants of Abraham, Isaac, and Jacob. God changed Jacob's name to "Israel," and Jacob's twelve sons and their children became the leaders of the twelve tribes of Israel. (*See* Hebrews.) [israelitas]

J

Jerusalem city conquered by David in 1000 B.C. to serve as his capital. David also made it the center of worship by bringing in the Ark of the Covenant, which held the tablets of the Law. [Jerusalén]

Jesse Tree an Advent activity that helps us to prepare to celebrate Jesus' birth. A small real or artificial tree is decorated with images of Jesus' ancestors beginning with Jesse of Bethlehem, father of King David. The image is based on Isaiah 11:1 *But a shoot shall sprout from the stump of Jesse, and from his roots a bud shall blossom.* [tronco de Jesé]

Jesus the Son of God, who was born of the Virgin Mary and who died and was raised from the dead for our Salvation. He returned to God and will come again to judge the living and the dead. *Jesus* means "God saves." [Jesús]

Jews the name given to the Hebrew people, from the time of the exile to the present. The name means "the people who live in the territory of Judah," the area of Palestine surrounding Jerusalem. [judíos]

Joseph the foster father of Jesus, who was engaged to Mary when the angel announced that Mary would have a child through the power of the Holy Spirit. In the Old Testament, Joseph was the son of Jacob, who was sold into slavery in Egypt by his brothers and then saved them from starvation when famine came. [José]

Judaism the name of the religion of Jesus and all of the people of Israel after they returned from exile in Babylon and built the second Temple [judaísmo]

justice the virtue that guides us to give to God and others what is due them. Justice is one of the four central human virtues, called the cardinal virtues, by which we guide our Christian life. [justicia]

K

Kingdom of God God's rule over us, announced in the Gospel and present in the Eucharist. The beginning of the Kingdom here on earth is mysteriously present in the Church, and it will come in completeness at the end of time. [reino de Dios]

Kingdom of Heaven the Gospel of Matthew's term for the Kingdom of God. The Kingdom of God is God's rule over us, announced in the Gospel and present in the Eucharist. [reino de los cielos]

knowledge one of the seven Gifts of the Holy Spirit. This gift helps us to know what God asks of us and how we should respond. [conocimiento]

L

laity those who have been made members of Christ in Baptism and who participate in the priestly, prophetic, and kingly functions of Christ in his mission to the whole world. The laity is distinct from the clergy, whose members are set apart as ministers to serve the Church. [laicado]

Lamb of God the title for Jesus that emphasizes his willingness to give up his life for the Salvation of the world. Jesus is the Lamb without blemish or sin who delivers us through his sacrificial Death. [cordero de Dios]

Last Supper the last meal Jesus ate with his disciples on the night before he died. At the Last Supper, Jesus took bread and wine, blessed them, and said that they were his Body and Blood. Jesus' Death and Resurrection, which we celebrate in the Eucharist, was anticipated in this meal. [Última Cena]

Lectionary for Mass the official book that contains all the Scripture readings used in the Liturgy of the Word [Leccionario]

Lent the 40 days before Easter (not counting Sundays) during which we prepare, through prayer, fasting, and giving aid to those who are poor, to change our lives and live the Gospel more completely [Cuaresma]

Light of the World a name that helps us see that Jesus is the light that leads us to the Father. Jesus lights up our minds and hearts, replacing sin and darkness with the knowledge of God. [luz del mundo]

liturgical year the celebration throughout the year of the mysteries of the Lord's birth, life, Death, Resurrection, and Ascension. The cycle of the liturgical year constitutes the basic rhythm of the Christian's life of prayer. [año litúrgico]

liturgy the public prayer of the Church that celebrates the wonderful things God has done for us in Jesus Christ, our high priest, and the way in which he continues the work of our Salvation. The original meaning of *liturgy* was "a public work or service done for the people." [liturgia]

Liturgy of the Eucharist the part of the Mass in which the bread and wine are consecrated and become the Body and Blood of Jesus Christ. We then receive Christ in Holy Communion. [Liturgia de la Eucaristía]

Liturgy of the Hours the public prayer of the Church to praise God and sanctify the day. It includes an office of readings before sunrise, morning prayer at dawn, evening prayer at sunset, and prayer before going to bed. The chanting of psalms makes up a major portion of each of these services. [Liturgia de las Horas]

Liturgy of the Word the part of the Mass in which we listen to God's Word from the Bible and consider what it means for us today. The Liturgy of the Word can also be a public prayer and proclamation of God's Word that is not followed by the Liturgy of the Eucharist. [Liturgia de la Palabra]

M

Magisterium the living, teaching office of the Church. This office, through the bishops and with the pope, provides an authentic interpretation of the Word of God. It ensures faithfulness to the teaching of the apostles in matters of faith and morals. [Magisterio]

Magnificat Mary's song of praise to God for the great things he has done for her and for his plans for us through Jesus [Magníficat]

manna the food provided by God when the Israelites were in the desert [maná]

Marks of the Church the four most important aspects of the Church found in the Nicene Creed. According to the Nicene Creed, the Church is one, holy, catholic, and apostolic. [atributos de la Iglesia]

Mary the mother of Jesus. She is called blessed and "full of grace" because God chose her to be the mother of the Son of God, the second Person of the Trinity. [María]

Mass the most important sacramental celebration of the Church, established by Jesus at the Last Supper as a remembrance of his Death and Resurrection. At Mass we listen to God's Word from the Bible and receive Jesus Christ in the consecrated Bread and Wine that are his Body and Blood. [misa]

Matrimony a solemn agreement between a woman and a man to be partners for life, both for their own good and for raising children. Marriage is a sacrament when the agreement is properly made between baptized Christians. [Matrimonio]

memorial a remembrance of events that have taken place in the past. We recall these events because they continue to affect us because they are part of God's saving plan for us. Every time we remember these events, we make God's saving action present. [conmemoración]

mercy the gift to be able to respond to those in need with care and compassion. The gift of mercy is a grace given to us by Jesus Christ. [misericordia]

Messiah a title that means "anointed with oil." It is from a Hebrew word that means the same thing as the Greek word *Christ*. "Messiah" is the title that was given to Jesus after the Resurrection, when he had completed his mission as priest, prophet, and king. [Mesías]

ministry service or work done for others. Ministry is done by bishops, priests, and deacons, who are all ordained to ministry in the celebration of the sacraments. All those baptized are called to a variety of ministries in the liturgy and in service to the needs of others. [ministerio]

miracle the healing of a person, or an occasion when nature is controlled that can only be recognized as God's action in the world. Jesus' miracles are signs of the presence of God's kingdom. [milagro]

mission the work of Jesus Christ that is continued in the Church through the Holy Spirit. The mission of the Church is to proclaim Salvation in Jesus' life, Death, Resurrection, and Ascension. [misión]

monastery a place where men or women live out their solemn vows of poverty, chastity, and obedience in a stable community life. They spend their days in public prayer, work, and meditation. [monasterio]

moral choice a choice to do what is right or not do what is wrong. We make moral choices because they help us grow closer to God and because we have the freedom to choose what is right and avoid what is wrong. [opción moral]

moral law a rule for living that has been established by God and people in authority who are concerned about the good of all. Moral laws are based on God's direction to us to do what is right and avoid what is wrong. Some moral laws are "written" in the human heart and can be known through our own reasoning. Other moral laws have been revealed to us by God in the Old Testament and in the new Law given by Jesus. [ley moral]

mortal sin a decision to turn away from God by doing something that we know is seriously wrong. For a sin to be mortal, it must be a very serious offense, the person must know how serious the sin is, and the person must freely choose to do it anyway. [pecado mortal]

Muslim a follower of the religion of Islam. *Muslim* means "one who submits to God." [musulmán]

mystery a religious truth that we can know only through God's revelation and that we cannot fully understand. Our faith is a mystery that we profess in the Creed and celebrate in the liturgy and sacraments. [misterio]

Mystical Body of Christ the members of the Church formed into a spiritual body and bound together by the life communicated by Jesus Christ through the sacraments. Christ is the center of this body and the source of life. In it we are all united. Each member of the body receives from Christ gifts fitting for him or her. [Cuerpo Místico de Cristo]

N

Nativity scene a picture or crèche that shows Jesus, Mary, and Joseph in the stable after the birth of Jesus as described in the Gospels of Matthew and Luke [escena de la Natividad del Señor]

natural law the moral law that is "written" in the human heart. We can know natural law through our own reason because the Creator has placed the knowledge of it in our hearts. It can provide the solid foundation on which we can make rules to guide our choices in life. Natural law forms the basis of our fundamental rights and duties and is the foundation for the work of the Holy Spirit in guiding our moral choices. [ley natural]

neighbor according to Jesus, everyone, as each person is made in God's image. We are all meant to develop mutually supportive relationships. [prójimo]

New Testament the 27 books of the second part of the Bible which tell of the teaching, ministry, and saving events of the life of Jesus. The four Gospels present Jesus' life, Death, and Resurrection. The Acts of the Apostles tells the story of Jesus' Ascension into Heaven. It also shows how Jesus' message of Salvation spread through the growth of the Church. Various letters instruct us in how to live as followers of Jesus Christ. The Book of Revelation offers encouragement to Christians living through persecution. [Nuevo Testamento]

Nicene Creed the summary of Christian beliefs developed by the bishops at the first two councils of the Church, held in A.D. 325 and 381. It is the Creed shared by most Christians in the East and in the West. [Credo Niceno]

O

obedience the act of willingly following what God asks us to do for our Salvation. The Fourth Commandment requires children to obey their parents, and all people are required to obey civil authority when it acts for the good of all. To imitate the obedience of Jesus, members of religious communities make a special vow of obedience. [obediencia]

obey to follow the teachings or directions given by God or by someone who has authority over us [obedecer]

oil of catechumens the oil blessed by the bishop during Holy Week and used to anoint catechumens. This anointing strengthens them on their path to initiation into the Church. Infants are anointed with this oil right before they are baptized. [óleo de los catecúmenos]

oil of the sick the oil blessed by the bishop during Holy Week and used in the Sacrament of the Anointing of the Sick, which brings spiritual and, if it is God's will, physical healing [óleo de los enfermos]

Old Testament the first 46 books of the Bible, which tell of God's Covenant with the people of Israel and his plan for the Salvation of all people. The first five books are known as the Torah. The Old Testament is fulfilled in the New Testament, but God's Covenant presented in the Old Testament has permanent value and has never been revoked. [Antiguo Testamento]

one one of the four Marks of the Church. The Church is one because of its source in the one God and because of its founder, Jesus Christ. Jesus, through his Death on the cross, united all to God in one body. Within the unity of the Church, there is great diversity because of the variety of the gifts given to its members. [una]

ordained men who have received the Sacrament of Holy Orders so that they may preside at the celebration of the Eucharist and serve as leaders and teachers of the Church [ordenado]

Ordinary Time the longest liturgical season of the Church. It is divided into two periods—the first after the Christmas season and the second after Pentecost. The first period focuses on Jesus' childhood and public ministry. The second period focuses on Christ's reign as King of Kings. [Tiempo Ordinario]

ordination the rite of the Sacrament of Holy Orders, by which a bishop gives to men, through the laying on of hands, the ability to minister to the Church as bishops, priests, and deacons [ordenación]

Original Sin the consequence of the disobedience of the first human beings. They disobeyed God and chose to follow their own will rather than God's will. As a result human beings lost the original blessing God had intended and became subject to sin and death. In Baptism we are restored to life with God through Jesus Christ although we still experience the effects of Original Sin. [pecado original]

P

Palm Sunday the celebration of Jesus' triumphant entry into Jerusalem on the Sunday before Easter. It begins a week-long commemoration of the saving events of Holy Week. [Domingo de Ramos]

parable one of the simple stories that Jesus told to show us what the Kingdom of God is like. Parables present images drawn from everyday life. These images show us the radical choice we make when we respond to the invitation to enter the Kingdom of God. [parábola]

parish a stable community of believers in Jesus Christ who meet regularly in a specific area to worship God under the leadership of a pastor [parroquia]

Paschal Mystery the work of Salvation accomplished by Jesus Christ through his Passion, Death, and Resurrection. The Paschal Mystery is celebrated in the liturgy of the Church, and its saving effects are experienced by us in the sacraments. [Misterio Pascual]

Passion the suffering and Death of Jesus [pasión]

Passover the Jewish festival that commemorates the delivery of the Hebrew people from slavery in Egypt. In the Eucharist, we celebrate our passover from death to life through Jesus' Death and Resurrection. [Pascua Judía]

pastor a priest who is responsible for the spiritual care of the members of a parish community. It is the job of the pastor to see that the Word of God is preached, the faith is taught, and sacraments are celebrated. [pastor]

patriarchs the leaders of families and clans within ancient Israel. More specifically, in biblical studies, patriarchs are the founders of the Hebrew people described in Genesis chapters 12 through 50. Prominent among the patriarchs are Abraham, Isaac, Jacob, and Jacob's 12 sons. [patriarcas]

peacemaker a person who teaches us to be respectful in our words and actions toward one another [paz, los que trabajar por la]

penance the turning away from sin with a desire to change our life and more closely live the way God wants us to live. We express our penance externally by praying, fasting, and helping those who are poor. This is also the name of the action that the priest asks us to take or the prayers that he asks us to pray after he absolves us in the Sacrament of Penance and Reconciliation. (*See* Sacrament of Penance and Reconciliation.) [penitencia]

Penitential Act a formula of general confession asking for God's mercy said at Mass. The priest may lead the assembly in praying the *Confiteor* ("I confess to almighty God . . .") or a threefold invocation echoed by "Lord have mercy . . . Christ have mercy . . . Lord have mercy" in English or in Greek. [acto penitencial]

Pentecost the 50th day after Jesus was raised from the dead. On this day the Holy Spirit was sent from Heaven, and the Church was born. It is also the Jewish feast that celebrated the giving of the Ten Commandments on Mount Sinai 50 days after the Exodus. [Pentecostés]

People of God another name for the Church. In the same way that the people of Israel were God's people through the Covenant he made with them, the Church is a priestly, prophetic, and royal people through the new and eternal covenant with Jesus Christ. [pueblo de Dios]

personal prayer the kind of prayer that rises up in us in everyday life. We pray with others in the liturgy, but in addition we can listen and respond to God through personal prayer every moment of our lives. [oración personal]

personal sin a sin we choose to commit, whether serious (mortal) or less serious (venial). Although the consequences of Original Sin leave us with a tendency to sin, God's grace, especially through the sacraments, helps us to choose good over sin. [pecado personal]

petition a request to God, asking him to fulfill a need. When we share in God's saving love, we understand that every need is one that we can ask God to help us with through petition. [petición]

Pharaoh the Egyptian word for "Great House," referring to the royal palace of the king of Egypt. Then references to *Pharaoh* became known for the king himself, just as "White House" might refer to the president. Pharaoh was both the political and religious leader of Egypt. [faraón]

piety one of the seven Gifts of the Holy Spirit. This gift calls us to be faithful in our relationships both with God and with others. Piety helps us to love God and to behave responsibly and with generosity and affection toward others. [piedad]

plague a natural calamity or disease that is seen as being inflicted by God as a remedial event to make people more conscious of their duties toward God and one another. (Numbers 14:37) In Exodus 7:14—12:30, the plagues inflicted on the Egyptians are seen as the means by which God convinced the Egyptians to free the Hebrew people from slavery [plaga]

pope the bishop of Rome, successor of Saint Peter, and leader of the Roman Catholic

Church. Because he has the authority to act in the name of Christ, the pope is called the Vicar of Christ. The pope and all of the bishops together make up the living, teaching office of the Church, the Magisterium. [Papa]

praise the expression of our response to God, not only for what he does, but simply because he is. In the Eucharist the whole Church joins with Jesus Christ in expressing praise and thanksgiving to the Father. [alabanza]

prayer the raising of our hearts and minds to God. We are able to speak to and listen to God in prayer because he teaches us how to pray. [oración]

Precepts of the Church those positive requirements that the pastoral authority of the Church has determined are necessary to provide a minimum effort in prayer and the moral life. The Precepts of the Church ensure that all Catholics move beyond the minimum by growing in love of God and love of neighbor. [preceptos de la Iglesia]

presbyter a word that originally meant "an elder or a trusted advisor to the bishop." From this word comes the English word *priest*, one of the three degrees of the Sacrament of Holy Orders. All the priests of a diocese under the bishop form the presbyterate. [presbítero]

pride a false image of ourselves that goes beyond what we deserve as God's creation. Pride puts us in competition with God. It is one of the seven capital sins. [soberbia]

priest a man who has accepted God's special call to serve the Church by guiding it and building it up through the ministry of the Word and the celebration of the sacraments [sacerdote]

priesthood all the people of God who have been given a share of the one mission of Christ through the Sacraments of Baptism and Confirmation. The ministerial priesthood, which is made up of those men who have been ordained bishops and priests in Holy Orders, is essentially different from the priesthood of all the faithful because its work is to build up and guide the Church in the name of Christ. [sacerdocio]

Promised Land the land first promised by God to Abraham. It was to this land that God told Moses to lead the Chosen People after they were freed from slavery in Egypt and received the Ten Commandments at Mount Sinai. [Tierra prometida]

prophet one called to speak for God and call the people to be faithful to the Covenant. A major section of the Old Testament presents, in 18 books, the messages and actions of the prophets. [profeta]

prudence the virtue that directs us toward the good and helps us to choose the correct means to achieve that good. When we act with prudence, we carefully and thoughtfully consider our actions. Prudence is one of the cardinal virtues that guide our conscience and influence us to live according to the Law of Christ. [prudencia]

psalm a prayer in the form of a poem, written to be sung in public worship. Each psalm expresses an aspect of the depth of human prayer. Over several centuries 150 psalms were assembled into the Book of Psalms in the Old Testament. Psalms were used in worship in the Temple in Jerusalem, and they have been used in the public worship of the Church since its beginning. [salmo]

Purgatory a state of final cleansing after death of all of our human imperfections to prepare us to enter into the joy of God's presence in Heaven [purgatorio]

R

racism the opinion that race determines human traits and capacities and that a particular race has an inherent, or inborn, superiority. Discrimination based on a person's race is a violation of human dignity and a sin against justice. [racismo]

Real Presence the way in which the risen Jesus Christ is present in the Eucharist under the form of Bread and Wine. Jesus Christ's presence is called real because in the Eucharist his Body and Blood, soul and divinity, are wholly and entirely present. [Presencia Real]

reconciliation the renewal of friendship after that friendship has been broken by some action or lack of action. In the Sacrament of Penance and Reconciliation, through God's mercy and forgiveness, we are reconciled with God, the Church, and others. [reconciliación]

Redeemer Jesus Christ, whose life, sacrificial Death on the cross, and Resurrection from the dead set us free from the slavery of sin and bring us redemption [Redentor]

redemption our being set free from the slavery of sin through the life, sacrificial Death on the cross, and Resurrection from the dead of Jesus Christ [redención]

reform to put an end to a wrong by introducing a better or changed course of action. The prophets called people to reform their lives by returning to being faithful to their Covenant with God. [reformarse]

religious life a state of life recognized by the Church. In the religious life, men and women freely respond to a call to follow Jesus by living the vows of poverty, chastity, and obedience in community with others. [vida religiosa]

repentance our turning away from sin with a desire to change our lives and live more closely as God wants us to live. We express our penance externally by prayer, fasting, and helping those who are poor. [arrepentimiento]

Resurrection the bodily raising of Jesus Christ from the dead on the third day after his Death on the cross. The Resurrection is the crowning truth of our faith. [Resurrección]

Revelation God's communication of himself to us through the words and deeds he has used throughout history to show us the mystery of his plan for our Salvation. This revelation reaches its completion in his sending of his Son, Jesus Christ. [revelación]

rite one of the many forms followed in celebrating liturgy in the Church. A rite may differ according to the culture or country where it is celebrated. *Rite* also means "the special form for celebrating each sacrament." [rito]

Rosary a prayer in honor of the Blessed Virgin Mary. When we pray the Rosary, we meditate on the mysteries of Jesus Christ's life while praying the Hail Mary on five sets of ten beads and the Lord's Prayer on the beads in between. In the Latin Church, praying the Rosary became a way for ordinary people to reflect on the mysteries of Christ's life. [Rosario]

S

Sabbath the seventh day, when God rested after finishing the work of Creation. The Third Commandment requires us to keep the Sabbath holy. For Christians the Sabbath became Sunday because it was the day Jesus rose from the dead and the new creation in Jesus Christ began. [Sabat]

sacrament one of seven ways through which God's life enters our lives through the work of the Holy Spirit. Jesus gave us three sacraments that bring us into the Church: Baptism, Confirmation, and the Eucharist. He gave us two sacraments that bring us healing: Penance and Reconciliation and Anointing of the Sick. He also gave us two sacraments that help members serve the community: Matrimony and Holy Orders. [sacramento]

sacramental an object, a prayer, or a blessing given by the Church to help us grow in our spiritual life [sacramental]

Sacrament of Penance and Reconciliation the sacrament in which we celebrate God's forgiveness of sin and our reconciliation with God and the Church. Penance includes sorrow for the sins we have committed, confession of sins, absolution by the priest, and doing the penance that shows our willingness to amend our ways. [sacramento de la Penitencia y de la Reconciliación]

Sacraments at the Service of Communion the Sacraments of Holy Orders and Matrimony. These two sacraments contribute to the personal Salvation of individuals by giving them a way to serve others. [sacramentos al servicio de la comunidad]

Sacraments of Healing the Sacraments of Penance and Reconciliation and Anointing of the Sick, by which the Church continues the healing ministry of Jesus for soul and body [sacramentos de curación]

Sacraments of Initiation the sacraments that are the foundation of our Christian life. We are born anew in Baptism, strengthened by Confirmation, and receive in the Eucharist the food of eternal life. By means of these sacraments, we receive an increasing measure of divine life and advance toward the perfection of charity. [sacramentos de iniciación]

sacrifice a ritual offering of animals or produce made to God by the priest in the Temple in Jerusalem. Sacrifice was a sign of the people's adoration of God, giving thanks to God, or asking for his forgiveness. Sacrifice also showed union with God. The great high priest, Christ, accomplished our redemption through the perfect sacrifice of his Death on the cross. [sacrificio]

Sacrifice of the Mass the sacrifice of Jesus on the cross, which is remembered and mysteriously made present in the Eucharist. It is offered in reparation for the sins of the living and the dead and to obtain spiritual or temporal blessings from God. [Sacrificio de la misa]

saint a holy person who has died united with God. The Church has said that this person is now with God forever in Heaven. [santo]

Salvation the gift, which God alone can give, of forgiveness of sin and the restoration of friendship with him [salvación]

sanctifying grace the gift of God, given to us without our earning it, that unites us with the life of the Trinity and heals our human nature, wounded by sin. Sanctifying grace continues the work of making us holy that began at our Baptism. [gracia santificante]

Savior Jesus, the Son of God, who became man to forgive our sins and restore our friendship with God. *Jesus* means "God saves." [Salvador]

scriptorium the room in a monastery in which books were copied by hand. Often, beautiful art was created on the page to illustrate the story. [scriptorium]

Scriptures the holy writings of Jews and Christians collected in the Old and New Testaments of the Bible [Sagrada Escritura]

seal of confession also called the "sacramental seal." It declares that the priest is absolutely forbidden to reveal under any circumstances any sin confessed to him in the Sacrament of Penance and Reconciliation. [sigilo sacramental]

seraphim the Heavenly beings who worship before the throne of God. One of them purified the lips of Isaiah with a burning coal so that he could speak for God (Isaiah 6:6–7). [serafines]

Sermon on the Mount the words of Jesus, written in chapters 5 through 7 of the Gospel of Matthew, in which Jesus reveals how he has fulfilled God's Law given to Moses. The Sermon on the Mount begins with the eight Beatitudes and includes the Lord's Prayer. [Sermón de la montaña]

sexism a prejudice or discrimination based on sex, especially discrimination against women. Sexism leads to behaviors and attitudes that foster a view of social roles based only on sex. [sexismo]

Sign of Peace the part of the Mass in which we offer a gesture of peace to one another as we prepare to receive Holy Communion. This signifies our willingness to be united in peace before we receive our Lord. [rito de la paz]

Sign of the Cross the gesture that we make that signifies our belief in God the Father, the Son, and the Holy Spirit. It is a sign of blessing, a confession of faith, and identifies us as followers of Jesus Christ. [señal de la cruz]

sin a deliberate thought, word, deed, or failure to act that offends God and hurts our relationships with other people. Some sin is mortal and needs to be confessed in the Sacrament of Penance and Reconciliation. Other sin is venial, or less serious. [pecado]

slander a false statement that harms the reputation of someone and makes other people think badly of that person. Slander is an offense against the Eighth Commandment. [calumnia]

sloth a carelessness of heart that leads a person to ignore his or her development as a person, especially spiritual development and a relationship with God. Sloth is one of the seven capital sins, and it is contrary to the First Commandment. [pereza]

solidarity the principle that all people exist in equal dignity as children of God. Therefore, individuals are called to commit themselves to working for the common good in sharing material and spiritual goods. [solidaridad]

Son of God the title revealed by Jesus that indicates his unique relationship to God the Father. The revelation of Jesus' divine sonship is the main dramatic development of the story of Jesus of Nazareth as it unfolds in the Gospels. [Hijo de Dios]

soul the part of us that makes us human and an image of God. Body and soul together form one unique human nature. The soul is responsible for our consciousness and for our freedom. The soul does not die and is reunited with the body in the final resurrection. [alma]

Spiritual Works of Mercy the kind acts through which we help our neighbors meet needs that are more than material. The Spiritual Works of Mercy include instructing, advising, consoling, comforting, forgiving, and bearing wrongs with patience. [obras espirituales de misericordia]

Stations of the Cross a tool for meditating on the final hours of Jesus' life, from his condemnation by Pilate to his Death and burial. We do this by moving to representations of 14 incidents, each one based on the traditional sites in Jerusalem where these incidents took place. [Estaciones del Vía Crucis]

stewardship the careful and responsible management of something entrusted to one's care, especially the goods of creation, which are intended for the whole human race. The sixth Precept of the Church makes clear our part in this stewardship by requiring us to provide for the material needs of the Church, according to our abilities. [administración]

T

tabernacle the container in which the Blessed Sacrament is kept so that Holy Communion can be taken to those who are sick and dying. *Tabernacle* is also the name of the tent sanctuary in which the Israelites kept the Ark of the Covenant from the time of the Exodus to the construction of Solomon's Temple. [sagrario]

temperance the cardinal virtue that helps us to control our attraction to pleasure so that our natural desires are kept within proper limits. This moral virtue helps us choose to use created goods in moderation. [templanza]

Temple the house of worship of God, first built by Solomon. The Temple provided a place for the priests to offer sacrifice, to adore and give thanks to God, and to ask for forgiveness. It was destroyed and rebuilt. The second Temple was also destroyed and was never rebuilt. Part of the outer wall of the Temple mount remains to this day in Jerusalem. [Templo, judío]

temptation an attraction, from outside us or inside us, that can lead us to disobey God's commands. Everyone is tempted, but the Holy Spirit helps us to resist temptation and choose to do good. [tentación]

Ten Commandments the ten rules given by God to Moses on Mount Sinai that sum up God's Law and show us what is required to love God and our neighbor. By following the Ten Commandments, the Hebrews accepted their Covenant with God. [Diez Mandamientos]

Theological Virtues those virtues given us by God and not by human effort. They are faith, hope, and charity. [virtudes teologales]

Torah the Hebrew word for "instruction" or "law." It is also the name of the first five books of the Old Testament: Genesis, Exodus, Leviticus, Numbers, and Deuteronomy. [Torá]

transubstantiation when the bread and wine become the Body and Blood of Jesus Christ. When the priest speaks the words of consecration, the substance of the bread and wine is changed into the substance of Christ's Body and Blood. [transubstanciación]

trespasses unlawful acts committed against the property or rights of another person or acts that physically harm a person [ofensas]

Trinity the mystery of the existence of God in three Persons: the Father, the Son, and the Holy Spirit. Each Person is God, whole and entire. Each is distinct only in the relationship of each to the others. [Trinidad]

U

understanding one of the seven Gifts of the Holy Spirit. This gift helps us make the right choices in life and in our relationships with God and with others. [entendimiento]

universal Church the entire Church as it exists throughout the world. The people of every diocese, along with their bishops and the pope, make up the universal Church. [Iglesia universal]

V

venial sin a choice we make that weakens our relationships with God or with others. Venial sin wounds and lessens the divine life in us. If we make no effort to do better, venial sin can lead to more serious sin. Through our participation in the Eucharist, venial sin is forgiven, strengthening our relationships with God and with others. [pecado venial]

viaticum the Eucharist that a dying person receives. It is spiritual food for the last journey we make as Christians, the journey through death to eternal life. [viático]

Vicar of Christ the title given to the pope who, as the successor of Saint Peter, has the authority to act in Christ's place. A vicar is someone who stands in for and acts for another. [Vicario de Cristo]

virtue an attitude or a way of acting that enables us to do good [virtud]

Visitation Mary's visit to Elizabeth to share the good news that Mary is to be the mother of Jesus. Elizabeth's greeting of Mary forms part of the Hail Mary. During this visit Mary sings the Magnificat, her praise of God. [Visitación]

vocation the call each of us has in life to be the person God wants us to be and the way we each serve the Church and the Kingdom of God. Each of us can live out his or her vocation as a layperson, as a member of a religious community, or as a member of the clergy. [vocación]

vow a deliberate and free promise made to God by people who want especially to dedicate their lives to God. Their vows give witness now to the kingdom that is to come. [voto]

Vulgate the Latin translation of the Bible by Saint Jerome from the Hebrew and Greek in which it was originally written. Most Christians of Saint Jerome's day no longer spoke Hebrew or Greek. The common language, or vulgate, was Latin. [Vulgata]

W

wisdom one of the seven Gifts of the Holy Spirit. Wisdom helps us to understand the purpose and plan of God and to live in a way that helps to bring about this plan. It begins in wonder and awe at God's greatness. [sabiduría]

Wisdom Literature the Old Testament books of Job, Proverbs, Ecclesiastes, the Song of Songs, Wisdom, and Sirach. The purpose of these books is to give instruction on ways to live and how to understand and cope with the problems of life. [Libros Sapienciales]

witness the passing on to others, by our words and by our actions, the faith that we have been given. Every Christian has the duty to give witness to the good news about Jesus Christ that he or she has come to know. [testimonio]

worship the adoration and honor given to God in public prayer [culto]

Y

Yahweh the name of God in Hebrew, which God told Moses from the burning bush. *Yahweh* means "I am who am" or "I cause to be all that is." [Yavé]

Index

Acknowledgments

Excerpts from the *New American Bible with Revised New Testament and Psalms.* Copyright © 1991, 1986, 1970 Confraternity of Christian Doctrine, Inc., Washington, DC. Used with permission. All rights reserved. No part of the *New American Bible* may be reprinted without permission in writing from the copyright holder.

The English translation of the Act of Contrition from *Rite of Penance* © 1974, International Commission on English in the Liturgy Corporation (ICEL); the English translation of the *Salve, Regina* from *A Book of Prayers* © 1982, ICEL; the English translation of Prayer Before Meals and Prayer After Meals from *Book of Blessings* © 1988; the English translation of the Nicene Creed and Apostles' Creed from *The Roman Missal* © 2010, ICEL. All rights reserved.

The English translation of the *Magnificat* by the International Consultation on English Texts.

For more information related to the English translation of the *Roman Missal, Third Edition,* see www.loyolapress.com/romanmissal.

Loyola Press has made every effort to locate the copyright holders for the cited works used in this publication and to make full acknowledgment for their use. In the case of any omissions, the publisher will be pleased to make suitable acknowledgments in future editions.

Art and Photography

When there is more than one picture on a page, positions are abbreviated as follows: (t) top, (c) center, (b) bottom, (l) left, (r) right, (bg) background, (bd) border.

Photos and illustrations not acknowledged are either owned by Loyola Press or from royalty-free sources including but not limited to Alamy, Corbis/Veer, Getty Images, Jupiterimages, PunchStock, Thinkstock, and Wikipedia Commons. Loyola Press has made every effort to locate the copyright holders for the cited works used in this publication and to make full acknowledgment for their use. In the case of any omissions, the publisher will be pleased to make suitable acknowledgments in future editions.

Frontmatter: i Raphael Lopez. **iii**(tl) ©iStockphoto.com/pixdeluxe. **iii**(tr) ©iStockphoto.com/BlackJack3D. **iii**(br) Jupiterimages/Comstock/Thinkstock. **iv** Clockwise from top, (a) Ghislain & Marie David de Lossy/cultura/Corbis. **iv**(b) ©iStockphoto.com/russellmcbride. **iv**(c) ©iStockphoto.com/EasyBuy4u. **iv**(d) Thomas Northcut/Photodisc/Thinkstock. **iv**(e) Rob Melnychuk/Digital Vision/Getty Images.

©iStockphoto.com: 5(t, b) mxtama. **7**(br) mxtama. **10**(b) Tomacco. **13**(c) jossdim. **16**(t) GlobalP. **19**(tl,b) appleuzr. **28**(l) DNY59. **28**(r) skeeg. **29**(b) rangepuppies. **30**(c) mxtama. **32**(t) spxChrome. **36** Osuleo. **37**(bg) gfxwork. **49** duckycards. **57**(tl) perets. **57**(tr) Zmiy. **60**(tl) BlackJack3D. **62**(t) fotoVoyager. **67**(b) tepic. **68**(t) dlerick. **68**(b) sugapopcandy. **76**(t) pixdeluxe. **79**(t) DistinctiveImages. **85**(t) JHLloyd. **85**(b) pixdeluxe. **87**(tr) miflippo. **88–89**(b) shaneillustration. **91**(t) stocksnapper. **96** ParkerDeen. **97**(t) Jbryson. **106–107**(b) EasyBuy4u. **107**(t) kryczka. **117**(t) skeeg. **118**(t) cathyclapper2. **121**(t) milosluz. **122**(b) perkmeup. **124**(t) wibs24. **124**(c) yuliang11. **124**(b) Likhitha. **124**(bg) dra_schwartz. **125**(t) o-che. **125**(b) stevegraham. **130**(t, bl) FreeTransform. **130**(bd) deeAuvil. **133**(bg) Cloudniners. **137**(b) Jbryson. **140**(t) marivlada. **142** ranplett. **145**(tl) mxtama. **146**(c) fotek. **147**(t) MarinaMM. **148**(t) manfredxy. **148**(c) noticelj. **148**(b) ekvals. **152**(bg) dra_schwartz. **154**(b) skilpad. **155**(br) ermek. **165**(t) skeeg. **166–167**(b) mxtama. **167**(t) pixdeluxe. **167**(r) chrisboy2004. **169**(t) mxtama. **169**(br) DanielBendjy. **171**(b) laflor. **172** botsman141. **173**(r) colematt. **180** kulicki. **181**(b) ajt. **183**(l) princessdlaf. **186**(bg) dra_schwartz. **197**(b) russellmcbride. **203**(b) duckycards. **207** Stratol. **208**(l) winterling. **208**(r) YuriSH. **211** wha4. **212**(l) slobo. **212**(r) sshepard. **215**(bd) dra_schwartz. **216**(t) LeggNet. **217** JBryson. **222**(b) hutale. **222–223**(c) Maljuk. **224**(bl) iStockphoto.com/linearcurveslinearcurves. **225**(b) LattaPictures. **232** Illustrious. **251** dem10.

Thinkstock: 26(b) Jupiterimages/Brand X Pictures. **30**(b) George Doyle/Valueline. **37**(b) Jupiterimages/Comstock. **45** Ryan McVay/Lifesize. **54** Thinkstock/Comstock. **70**(b) iStockphoto. **80**(b) Stockbyte/Valueline. **98**(t) Jupiterimages/Creatas. **98**(b) Jupiterimages/Comstock. **109**(r) Thomas Northcut/Photodisc. **114** John Howard/Lifesize. **127**(b) Hemera. **153**(t) iStockphoto. **157**(t) Hemera. **163**(t) Jupiterimages/Comstock. **188**(r) iStockphoto. **213**(t) Jupiterimages/Cornstock. **214** iStockphoto. **215**(t) Darrin Klimek/Lifesize. **215**(b) Andrew Olney/Digital Vision. **216**(bg) Hemera. **216**(ct) Jupiterimages/Brand X Pictures. **218–219**(bg) Hemera. **220–221**(bg) Hemera. **221**(r) Thomas Northcut/Photodisc. **223**(r) iStockphoto. **225**(t) Hemera. **226**(b) iStockphoto. **227**(b) Thomas Northcut/Photodisc. **228**(r) Thomas Northcut/Photodisc.

Unit 1: 1(t) Tom Grill/Corbis. **1**(b) St. Jerome in his Study (oil on linen paper on panel), Eyck, Jan van (c.1390–1441) (attr. to)/Detroit Institute of Arts, USA/City of Detroit Purchase/The Bridgeman Art Library International **2** St. Jerome in his Study (oil on linen paper on panel), Eyck, Jan van (c.1390–1441) (attr. to)/Detroit Institute of Arts, USA/City of Detroit Purchase/The Bridgeman Art Library International **3** Thinkstock LLC. **4**(b) Phil Martin Photography. **5**(c) Bibliotheque Sainte-Genevieve, Paris, France/Archives Charmet/The Bridgeman Art Library International. **6**(t) Jupiterimages. **6**(c) Shutterstock.com. **6**(b) Jupiterimages. **7**(tl) Jupiterimages. **7**(tr) Eugene Ivanov/Shutterstock.com. **7**(bl) Jupiterimages. **8**(c) Jupiterimages. **9** MM Productions/Corbis. **10**(t) David Diaz. **11**(t) The British Museum. **11**(c) ANP/Shutterstock.com. **11**(b) The Crosiers/Gene Plaisted, OSC. **12** Yellowj/Shutterstock.com. **13**(t) The Crosiers/Gene Plaisted, OSC. **14**(t) Ocean Photography/Veer. **14**(b) Muriel Frega/Alloy Illustration/Veer. **15** Alloy Photography/Veer. **16**(b) The Crosiers/Gene Plaisted, OSC. **17** The Crosiers/Gene Plaisted, OSC. **18** Don Hammond/Design Pics/Corbis. **19**(tr) Courtesy of Leonidas Orellano Castro, Peru/Phil Martin Photography. **20**(t) David Diaz. **20**(b) Moiss/Shutterstock.com. **21** Corbis Yellow/Corbis. **22** Abraham and the Three Angels (oil on canvas), Carracci, Lodovico (1555–1619)/Pinacoteca Nazionale, Bologna, Italy/Alinari/The Bridgeman Art Library International. **23** The Crosiers/Gene Plaisted, OSC. **24** Tim Hall/Corbis. **26**(t) The Crosiers/Gene Plaisted, OSC. **27** Phil Martin Photography. **29**(t) The Crosiers/Gene Plaisted, OSC. **30**(b) Stockbyte/Getty Images.

Unit 2: 31(t) ICP/Alamy. **31**(b) The Crosiers/Gene Plaisted, OSC. **32**(b) The Crosiers/Gene Plaisted, OSC. **32**(b) Donovan Reese. **33** David Young-Wolff/PhotoEdit. **34**(l) The Crosiers/Gene Plaisted, OSC. **34**(r) Jupiterimages. **35**(l) Private Collection/The Bridgeman Art Library International. **35**(r) Jupiterimages. **37**(t) Siede Preis/Photodisc. **38**(t) Mel Curtis/Photodisc. **38**(b) AVAVA/Shutterstock.com. **39** Purestock/Getty Images. **40** Scala/Art Resource, NY. **41** The Crosiers/Gene Plaisted, OSC. **42** Phil Martin Photography. **44**(t) Mitch Hrdlicka/photodisc/PictureQuest. **44**(b) Lou Cypher/Corbis. **46**(t) North Wind Picture Archives/Alamy. **46**(b) The Crosiers/Gene Plaisted, OSC. **47** Gianni Dagli Orti/Corbis. **48** Laurence Mouton/ès Photography/Corbis. **50**(t) The Crosiers/Gene Plaisted, OSC. **50**(b) Yuri Arcurs/Shutterstock.com. **51** Tanya Constantine/Blend Images/Corbis. **52–53**(b) Dejan Gileski/Shutterstock.com. **53**(t) The Crosiers/Gene Plaisted, OSC. **55**(t) Gino D'Achille. **56**(t) Robert Crawford. **56**(b) Digital Vision/Getty Images. **57**(b) Warling Studios. **58**(t) Graphische Sammlung Albertina, Vienna, Austria/The Bridgeman Art Library International. **58**(b) Alessandra Cimatoribus. **59** The Crosiers/Gene Plaisted, OSC. **60**(tr) Joe Mercier/Shutterstock.com. **60**(b) Phil Martin Photography.

Unit 3: 61(t) Atlantide Phototravel/Corbis. **61**(b) Francis G. Mayer/Corbis. **62**(t) Francis G. Mayer/Corbis. **63** Radius Images/Jupiterimages. **64**(t) Gino D'Achille **65**(b) Gino D'Achille **66** Design Pics Images. **69** RubberBall Photography/Veer. **70**(t) Photodisc. **71** Bildarchiv Preussischer Kulturbesitz/Art Resource. **72** Colorblind/Digital

Vision/Getty Images. **73** Alessandra Cimatoribus. **74**(t) Psalm 100, 2004 (acrylic on canvas), James, Laura (Contemporary Artist)/Private Collection/The Bridgeman Art Library International. **74**(b) Image Source Photography/Veer. **75** Tim Pannell/Corbis. **76–77**(b) Image Source/Corbis. **77**(t) David Diaz. **78** Ghislain & Marie David de Lossy/Corbis. **79**(bd) Jupiterimages. **79**(bg) Jupiterimages. **80**(t) Gordon Swanson/Shutterstock.com. **81** M.T.M. Images/Alamy. **82** The Crosiers/Gene Plaisted, OSC. **83**(t) The Crosiers/Gene Plaisted, OSC. **83**(b) W.P. Wittman Limited. **84** Blend Images Photography/Veer. **86**(b) Jeff Greenberg/Alamy. **87**(tl) Siede Preis/Photodisc. **87**(b) Blend Images Photography/Veer. **88**(t) The Crosiers/Gene Plaisted, OSC. **90**(t) Michael Moran, C.P. 2005. Photographed by Michael Skoglund, 2007. **90**(b) Brand X Pictures/PunchStock.

Unit 4: 91(b) The Crosiers/Gene Plaisted, OSC. **92**(t) The Crosiers/Gene Plaisted, OSC. **93** Tom Grill/Corbis. **94** Peter Siu. **95** The Crosiers/Gene Plaisted, OSC. **97**(b) Bettmann/Corbis. **99** Sharie Kennedy/Comet/Corbis. **100–101**(b) Gino D'Achille. **101**(t) The Crosiers/Gene Plaisted, OSC. **102** Ghislain & Marie David de Lossy/cultura/Corbis. **103** John Stevens. **104**(t) The Crosiers/Gene Plaisted, OSC. **104**(b) Warling Studios. **105** Greg Hinsdale/Comet/Corbis. **106**(t) W.P. Wittman Limited. **106**(c) Digital Vision/PunchStock. **108** Fancy/Alamy. **109**(bg) Jupiterimages. **110**(t) Digital Vision/PunchStock. **110**(b) Cherry Li/Anyone/amanaimages/Corbis. **111** Mika/zefa/Corbis. **112**(t) Laura James/Private Collection/The Bridgeman Art Library International. **112**(t) C Squared Studios/Photodisc. **112**(b) Jupiterimages. **113**(t) Jupiterimages. **113**(b) Warling Studios. **115** Warling Studios. **116**(t) Amos Morgan/Photodisc. **116**(b) Brand X Pictures/Jupiterimages. **117**(r) The Crosiers/Gene Plaisted, OSC. **118–119**(b) Christina Balit. **120**(t) The Palma Collection/Photodisc. **120**(b) Phil Martin Photography.

Unit 5: 121(b) Jan Spivy-Gilchrist/St. Benedict the African Parish. **122**(t) Jan Spivy-Gilchrist/St. Benedict the African Parish. **123** Fabrice Lerouge/Onoky/Corbis. **126** Gary John Norman/Getty Images. **127**(t) The Crosiers/Gene Plaisted, OSC. **128**(t) David Diaz. **128**(b) Redchopsticks Photography/Veer. **129** Hill Street Studios/Blend Images/Corbis. **130**(c) Buccina Studios/Valueline. **130**(b) Buccina Studios/Valueline. **131** Associated Press/Pier Paolo Cito. **132** Drew Myers/Fancy/Corbis. **133**(t) W.P. Wittman Limited. **133**(c) Digital Vision/Getty. **133**(b) W.P. Wittman Limited. **134**(t) MarioPonta/Alamy. **134**(b) Fancy Photography/Veer. **135** Klaus Tiedge/Fancy/Corbis. **136**(t) Johannes Kroemer/Corbis. **136**(b) Jupiterimages. **137**(t) Jupiterimages. **138** Karin Dreyer/Blend Images/Corbis. **139**(bg) Jupiterimages. **139**(b) Peter Siu. **140**(b) Golden Pixels LLC/Shutterstock.com. **141** Eric Fowke/Alamy. **143** Richard Levine/Alamy. **144** Ocean Photography/Corbis. **145**(tr) The Crosiers/Gene Plaisted, OSC. **146**(t) Warling Studios. **146**(b) Enigma/Alamy. **147**(b) Oleksiy Maksymenko/All Canada Photos/Corbis. **149** W.P. Wittman Limited. **150**(t) The Crosiers/Gene Plaisted, OSC. **150**(b) The Crosiers/Gene Plaisted, OSC.

Seasonal Sessions: 151 Julie Lonneman. **152** The Crosiers/Gene Plaisted, OSC. **153**(b) Warling Studios. **154**(t) Arte & Immagini srl/Corbis. **154**(c) Pshenichka/Shutterstock.com. **155**(t) Laurence Mouton/PhotoAlto/Corbis. **155**(bl) Triff/Shutterstock.com. **155**(bc) vesna cvorovic/Shutterstock.com. **155**(br) Tony Rothberg. **156** Tel Aviv Museum of Art, Israel/Gift of Georg Kareski/The Bridgeman Art Library International. **157**(cl) The Crosiers/Gene Plaisted, OSC. **157**(br) Warling Studios. **158** Galleria Querini-Stampalia, Venice, Italy/The Bridgeman Art Library International. **159** Dorling Kindersley Getty Images. **160** The Crosiers/Gene Plaisted, OSC. **161**(t) tanais/Shutterstock.com. **161**(l) Warling Studios. **161**(r) The Crosiers/Gene Plaisted, OSC. **162** James, Laura (Contemporary Artist)/Private Collection/The Bridgeman Art Library International. **163**(b) Jupiterimages. **164** HIP/Art Resource, NY. **165**(bl) Musee d'Art et d'Archeologie, Moulins, France/Giraudon/The Bridgeman Art Library International. **165**(br) Friedrich Stark/Alamy. **166**(c) Narodni Galerie, Prague, Czech Republic/Giraudon/The Bridgeman Art Library International. **167**(l) Moodboard Photography/Veer. **168** Images.com/Corbis. **169**(bl) Private Collection/The Bridgeman Art Library International. **170**(bg) Jupiterimages. **170**(b) Musee Conde, Chantilly, France/Giraudon/The Bridgeman Art Library International. **171**(t) The Crosiers/Gene Plaisted, OSC. **173**(t) Jupiterimages. **173**(l) Glasgow University Library, Scotland/The Bridgeman Art Library International.

173(bg) Jupiterimages. **174–175** Gino D'Achille. **176** The Crosiers/Gene Plaisted, OSC. **177** Louise Batalla Duran/Alamy. **178** The Crosiers/Gene Plaisted, OSC. **179**(l) Jupiterimages.

Endmatter: 181(tl) The Crosiers/Gene Plaisted, OSC. **181**(tr) Warling Studios. **182**(t) Warling Studios. **182–183**(b) Christina Balit. **183**(r) W.P. Wittman Limited. **184** The Crosiers/Gene Plaisted, OSC. **185** The Crosiers/Gene Plaisted, OSC. **185**(b) Kenneth Sponsler/Shutterstock.com. **186**(t) Blend Images Photography/Veer. **186**(c) Imagestate Media Partners Limited-Impact Photos/Alamy. **186**(b) Radius Images/Alamy. **187** JGI/Blend Images/Getty Images. **188–189**(bg) Kathleen Burke. **189**(r) IImage Source Photography/Veer. **190**(t) Marafona/Shutterstock.com. **190**(b) The Crosiers/Gene Plaisted, OSC. **190–191**(bg) Samiah Samin/Shutterstock.com. **191**(t) The Crosiers/Gene Plaisted, OSC. **192–193**(br, bl) The Crosiers/Gene Plaisted, OSC. **192–193**(bg) Konstanttin/Shutterstock.com. **193**(t) ImageZoo/Corbis. **193**(r) Warling Studios. **194** Chiesa di San Ilario, Bibbona, Tuscany, Italy/The Bridgeman Art Library International. **195** Greg Kuepfer. **196** The Crosiers/Gene Plaisted, OSC. **197**(t) The Crosiers/Gene Plaisted, OSC. **197**(c) The Crosiers/Gene Plaisted, OSC. **198–199** Zvonimir Atletic/Shutterstock.com. **200–201** Alessandra Cimatoribus. **202** W.P. Wittman Limited. **203**(tr) W.P. Wittman Limited. **203**(cr) W.P. Wittman Limited. **203**(br) W.P. Wittman Limited. **204**(b) The Crosiers/Gene Plaisted, OSC. **205**(t) Danita Delimont/Alamy. **206**(tl) The Crosiers/Gene Plaisted, OSC. **206**(tc) Kunsthistorisches Museum, Vienna, Austria/The Bridgeman Art Library International. **206**(tr) Louvre, Paris, France/Giraudon/The Bridgeman Art Library International. **206**(bl) Wang, Elizabeth (Contemporary Artist)/Private Collection/© Radiant Light/The Bridgeman Art Library International. **206**(bc) The Crosiers/Gene Plaisted, OSC. **206**(br) Private Collection/Photo © Boltin Picture Library/The Bridgeman Art Library International. **209**(tr) Warling Studios. **209**(cr) Warling Studios. **209**(br) Warling Studios. **209**(b) Rubberball/Corbis. **210** www.photodisc.com. **212**(b) Jupiterimages. **213**(b) Christina Balit. **215**(c) Alloy Photography/Veer. **216**(cb) Suzanne Tucker/Shutterstock.com. **216**(b) Warling Studios. **219**(r) Ocean/Corbis. **220**(bl) Getty Images/Digital Vision/James Woodson. **224**(br) Darius Ramazani/Corbis. **226**(t) Image Source/Corbis. **228**(l) Jupiterimages. **229** © Erich Lessing/Art Resource, NY. **230** Gino D'Achille. **231** © The Crosiers/Gene Plaisted, OSC. **233** © The Crosiers/Gene Plaisted OSC. **234** Gino D'Achille. **235** Janet McDonnell. **236** Gino D'Achille. **237** Gino D'Achille. **238** Royalty-free image (tree). **238** Veronica Maria Jarski (ornaments). **239** David Diaz. **240** © The Crosiers/Gene Plaisted, OSC. **241** Gino D'Achille. **242** Fran Gregory. **243** Jupiterimages. **244** David Diaz. **245** John Stevens. **246** Kantner's Illustrated Book of Objects. **247** Fran Gregory. **248** © The Crosiers/Gene Plaisted, OSC. **249** Wikipedia Commons. **250**(t) Hemera/Thinkstock. **252** © The Crosiers/Gene Plaisted, OSC. **253** Phil Martin Photography.